MW00639683

THE
COUNTERINSURGENCY
CHALLENGE

THE COUNTERINSURGENCY CHALLENGE

A Parable of Leadership and Decision Making in Modern Conflict

Christopher D. Kolenda
foreword by General Stanley A. McChrystal
(U.S. Army, Retired)

STACKPOLE
BOOKS

Copyright © 2012 by Christopher D. Kolenda

Published by
STACKPOLE BOOKS
5067 Ritter Road
Mechanicsburg, PA 17055
www.stackpolebooks.com

All rights reserved, including the right to reproduce this book or portions thereof
in any form or by any means, electronic or mechanical, including photocopying,
recording, or by any information storage and retrieval system, without permission in writing from the publisher. All inquiries should be addressed to Stackpole
Books, 5067 Ritter Road, Mechanicsburg PA 17055.

Printed in the United States of America
10 9 8 7 6 5 4 3 2 1
First edition

Cover design by Tessa J. Sweigert
Cover photo by Colin Anderson/Brand X Pictures/Getty Images

Library of Congress Cataloging-in-Publication Data

Kolenda, Christopher D.
  The counterinsurgency challenge : a parable of leadership and decision
making in modern conflict / Christopher D. Kolenda ; foreword by General
Stanley A. McChrystal (U.S. Army, Retired).
     p. cm.
  ISBN 978-0-8117-1177-7
  1. Counterinsurgency. 2. Tactics. 3. War—Decision making. 4. Counterinsurgency—Political aspects. 5. Computer war games—Fiction. 6. Didactic
literature. I. Title. II. Title: Parable of leadership and decision making in
modern conflict.
  U241.K65 2012
  355.02'18—dc23
                                   2012014023

*This book is dedicated to Tom Bostick, Dave Boris,
Ryan Fritsche, Adrian Hike, Chris Pfeifer, and Jacob Lowell—
brave men who died in combat under my command—
and to their families.
May the insights from this book honor their legacies,
their service, and their sacrifice.*

There are two laws that operate with iron consistency in counterinsurgency: the law of gravity . . . and the law of unintended consequences.

CONTENTS

FOREWORD

Much as Sir Ernest Swinton intended, as a young officer I read, and reread, his account of Lieutenant Backsight Forethought's empirical education in *The Defence of Duffer's Drift*. His description of a fictional battle during the Boer War was, and remains today, one of the most compelling approaches to explaining the complex lessons of military operations. Students of military history and strategy continue to study Swinton's account as they learn small-unit tactics. Lt. Forethought's iterative attempts to grasp the many factors contributing to his eventual success or failure were essential in demonstrating the dangers of some of the simplest, most tempting approaches.

Chris Kolenda takes the same approach to delve into counterinsurgency (COIN). At the heart of his text, Chris emphasizes that COIN is extraordinarily difficult. The need to understand the forces and motivations that drive the behavior of all the actors involved makes waging a successful COIN campaign an exercise in restraint and intelligence, as much as anything else.

While naturally difficult, COIN is made many times harder by cultural chasms between foreign counterinsurgents and the people living where the campaign is fought. The tendency is to oversimplify and define the problem in order to play to counterinsurgents' strengths (often military action). This is a dangerous trap—and one that counterinsurgent forces have fallen prey to time and time again over the course of history.

Chris demonstrates this unfortunate but natural tendency—as the narrator slowly peels back each layer of complexity, he discovers how much more there is to learn. Each step affirms that understanding and working though these natural cultural chasms is essential to a successful outcome.

As in Chris's first scenario, security forces in most historical insurgencies found themselves led into actions that alienated the population and strengthened the insurgency. As in judo—where a skilled practitioner leverages his opponent's weight and momentum to throw him—insurgents deftly "egg on" COIN forces into undermining their own efforts. They take actions that compel the counterinsurgent to use his most comfortable, but often least precise and least effective, tools: kinetic operations.

This is counterproductive. The way you conduct a war is often as important as the ends you seek. COIN forces must operate in a way that minimizes the negative impact on the people whose support they are pursuing. This means great care must be taken in every interaction—particularly when using violence. As the commander of U.S. and international forces in Afghanistan, I realized how we interacted with the Afghans—the way we drove and respected the culture, whether we knew and understood their language, and, above all, our efforts to prevent civilian causalities—were often the most difficult, and most important, of our tasks.

While COIN and human behavior are obviously complex, my experiences have confirmed that people tend to act rationally in their own interests, at least as far as they see them. Therefore, of all the requirements for success in COIN, "seeing" and "understanding" how the people define their interests is the most important. This demands establishing sources and conduits for the collection of information, followed by a rigorously open-minded approach to analysis. How you develop intelligence is challenging—military intelligence systems are designed to locate and assess the enemy, yet the most critical intelligence is actually how the population lives and thinks.

In reading Chris's work, I'd urge the reader to focus less on the "solution" that the narrator arrives at and more on the analytical process he moves through to get there. With each iteration, he knows more, and appreciates just how much more he doesn't know. He arrives at the essential humility that makes a leader self-confident enough to listen.

General Stanley A. McChrystal
(U.S. Army, Retired)

PREFACE

This book is a journey through the mind of a leader in combat. It explores how a commander, over a series of iterations, trial and error, learning, and adaptation, thinks through a highly complex, adaptive, and deadly environment—and how he uses that understanding to develop solutions tailored to the unique situation he faces on the ground.

In the context of the parable, the commander is forced to rethink his approach and decisions as he attempts to win. He even needs to rethink what it means to win.

At the practical level, the book is intended to promote critical thinking and examination of how well we prepare leaders and units for conflict in the real world. The parable serves as a mirror—and the image it reflects is not always flattering.

The U.S. military is without question the most tactically proficient and deadly force in the history of warfare. But such prowess is less relevant in counterinsurgency conflict than in conventional war. Individual exceptions aside, the U.S. military is often not very good at counterinsurgency.

At the more theoretical levels, the U.S. military needs to examine how it educates and develops leaders and organizations for conflict in the real world. Too many leaders are not mentally or psychologically equipped and prepared for the inevitable complexity and ambiguity. This is an institutional shortfall. This book is intended as one way to begin addressing the issue.

This book will be useful to military and civilian leaders operating in conflict areas, as well as anyone interested in understanding counterinsurgency. There is an emerging school of thought that suggests that the U.S. should no longer do counterinsurgency. Such a view is myopic. We cannot always choose the types of wars we must wage. Whether we wish it so or not, this kind of warfare and conflict seems likely to persist over the first half of the twenty-first century and beyond.

When faced with an insurgency, a combatant wages counterinsurgency. *How* the combatant choses to conduct the campaign is the critical determination.

Insurgencies are certainly not unique to this era—they have been used throughout history as a means for the "weak" (in conventional terms) to defeat the "strong." In this kind of warfare, pure military calculations rarely suffice. Political, social, economic, and cultural factors are generally more salient, and counterinsurgents ignore them at their own peril.

The United States military found itself dangerously ill-prepared for such conflicts in Afghanistan and Iraq—a persistent affliction. Myriad attempts to address the problem have helped, but we still too often find commanders applying linear, conventional thinking to nonlinear, unconventional problems—attempting military solutions to essentially political issues.

New doctrine for counterinsurgency has been useful, as has the rediscovery of decades-old books together with some recent works on the matter. Books from scholars and practitioners such as Galula, Nagl, Kilcullen, Kitson, and several others have advanced the American military's thinking. Professional military schools have finally begun devoting time to the subject (although lieutenants and captains arriving in my unit in Afghanistan as late as 2008 reported receiving little to no preparation for counterinsurgency). Combat training centers have improved. Graduate school for humanities disciplines, frowned upon in the 1990s, is now supported.

Nonetheless, the tendency to fall back on the perceived safety of conventional approaches continues. The U.S. military is not alone in the critically important pursuit of excellence in tactics, techniques, and procedures (TTPs). Perfect TTPs may win a firefight; alone, they are insufficient for successful counterinsurgency.

Doctrine and TTPs teach a military *what* to think. They are inadequate in developing the essential quality of *how* to think and adapt to uncertainty, ambiguity, and complexity. Theory, history, and the experiences of others are essential supplements to doctrine and personal experience. Critical thinking—the mental capital and courage to think through and understand the situation, challenge conventional wisdom, adapt to an ever-changing environment, and develop appropriate and even innovative solutions—is indispensable.

This short book seeks to illustrate the practical importance of critical thinking in counterinsurgency. The particular set of approaches that the commander comes to in this book in dealing with a unique set of circumstances is less important than the thought process he uses to determine them.

To debate the merits of the particulars as a checklist or recipe for success is to miss the entire point. Examining and debating the thinking and decision making, and using the parable as an entry point for evaluating actual situations, is the point.

In this parable, the reader follows the intellectual journey of a commander who attempts to apply what he has learned, to access what he has forgotten, to unlearn unhelpful dogma, and to open his mind to new ways of understanding. He does all this while grappling with a unique, deadly, and highly complex insurgency in a fictional place called Narabad Province in the country of Khanastan.

To make the point, I borrow the literary device made famous by British Major General Sir Ernest Dunlop Swinton in *The Defence of Duffer's Drift,* written when he was a captain in 1904. In *Duffer's Drift,* Swinton explores small-unit tactics through the mind of Lieutenant N. Backsight Forethought, who is engaged in a fictitious battle in the Boer War. The experience plays out over a series of six dreams, as "BF" fails, learns, and adapts, until he defends Duffer's Drift successfully.

This book is not the first to borrow Swinton's device, nor likely the last. Various books and professional military journal articles have done so as well. James McDonough's *The Defense of Hill 781,* a series of scenarios based on the U.S. Army's National Training Center, was an important part of my early professional development in conventional warfare. More recently, *The Defense of Jisr al-Doreaa* by Michael L. Burgoyne and Albert J. Marckwardt explores small-unit tactics in an urban environment in Iraq.

I have made a few important adaptations to the Swinton model. Instead of a series of dreams, the commander is placed in a simulation

that employs complex adaptive modeling to replicate an environment
and the myriad interactions that produce nonlinear outcomes—an important aspect of real war that neither the other works on counterinsurgency
nor combat training centers address adequately. After-action reviews at
the end of all but the last two scenarios help explain how these nonlinear
outcomes came about.

I also introduce two mentors for the commander: one he has been
close to for years, and one he has not. Mick Lundy is the prototypical
"TTP" commander—quite similar to many officers who grew up during
the 1980s and 1990s. Alexander Cross is Lundy's antithesis—a soldier-
scholar who suffered the penalty of being so before his time. In addition
to grappling with the scenario itself, the commander must also sort
through the often conflicting advice and counsel of his mentors. As the
commander learns, many of the ideas he had accepted as articles of faith
are revealed as false dogma. He also comes to appreciate that being a
commander involves dimensions of mental and moral courage he is only
now developing.

This book is a work of fiction. It is set in a country of my invention.
The characters have no connection with real ones. The specific events in
the book are entirely fictional, although I have seen or learned of similar
individual event outcomes that have occurred in places such as
Afghanistan and Iraq. I use them to illustrate the practical effects of non-
linearity and the unintended consequences when otherwise sound tactics
and procedures are applied with inadequate understanding of the environment.

Some Thoughts on Counterinsurgency

Counterinsurgency is not a strategy. Insurgency-counterinsurgency, like
conventional war, is a type of conflict. Strategy, as Carl von Clausewitz
tells us, must be based on understanding the nature of the specific conflict.

The point of counterinsurgency is to defeat the insurgency. I use the
term defeat to mean rendering the insurgency incapable of undermining
our national objectives. The nature of the conflict—the political, social,
economic, military, and cultural factors that interact to form it—must be
the foundation of strategy in counterinsurgency.

Counterinsurgents generally win—i.e., attain national objectives—in one of three ways: political victory, military victory, or favorable negotiated outcome (some combination of the three is most likely). A sound strategy or "theory of success" includes the "ways" to achieve national policy ends.

Counterinsurgency is a violent argument for the support of the people.

The political aspect is primary. A political victory occurs when the host government develops enough legitimacy and support or the insurgency undermines itself enough that the population turns against or isolates the insurgency. In cases where the insurgency is animated by an ideology the population does not support, the host government must gain legitimacy and support through the competition of ideas and the perceived practical outcomes of its efforts. Military force can secure the political victory but must be used in ways that do not undermine the legitimacy of the government in the eyes of the people.

In places where the insurgency is in a distinct geographic location and can be isolated from external sanctuary, a purely military victory against it is possible. It is also possible when the insurgency is isolated from the population. Both cases, however, require sufficient political success of the host nation as a precondition. In the first case, the host nation has sufficient political legitimacy in the rest of the country; in the second, political victory for the host government is imminent. Military force seals political success. When those conditions do not exist, a counterinsurgent must look to alternatives.

In cases where the insurgency is a popular revolt against the government across or in significantly large parts of the country, the host government will need to reform to earn legitimacy and support. The problem is that a government rarely does this on its own. Those in government often have too much at stake in the current (often corrupt) system to undertake reforms that would sacrifice such advantages. Even reform-minded leaders often lack the political will or capacity to implement corrective policy. In cases where the host government is too compromised and unable to summon the necessary political will and capacity, political victory will remain elusive.

Where military or political victory proves infeasible, the alternative is a favorable negotiated outcome. A negotiated outcome can be viewed as similar to a plea-bargain—neither party gains all it wants but both gain enough to satisfy key interests and stop the violent contest for power. One of the most critical decisions a counterinsurgent must make is when a favorable negotiated outcome is required. Too often, counterinsurgents fail to recognize when such a transition is necessary, or, when they do, they fail to adapt political and military efforts to bring it about. Combat and conflict have been described as the trading of military and political information. Over time, this information leads to assessments of likely outcomes on the military and political fronts. Cognitive bias, flawed assessments, and political pressures are among the factors that can either prolong a conflict that should be negotiated or result in premature negotiations and suboptimal outcomes.

A negotiated outcome can become a forcing function to generate necessary reforms that bring about a stable, inclusive, and resilient political order. To be sure, there are many ways a negotiated outcome can go wrong, and fewer ways it can go right. Negotiated outcomes can occur with entire insurgent groups or with factions among them. Such agreements may split an insurgency, in which reconcilable elements become part of the solution for political reform, while irreconcilable ones are isolated and more easily defeated politically or militarily.

Successful political reform will isolate the irreconcilables further. Once they are isolated from support, the prospect of military victory over them increases substantially.

Such outcomes must be inclusive, particularly in highly diverse and divided societies, and when external parties have proxies in-country. Otherwise, a settlement with one group can lead to spoiler activity, or worse, the trading of one conflict for another. Obstacles to a political process are often significant, creating trust and credibility gaps that must be addressed. The honor and dignity of all parties must be preserved. Enforcement mechanisms and proper incentive structures must be created to ensure that a favorable outcome remains durable.

Because insurgencies, especially rural ones in highly complex and compartmentalized terrain, can take on very unique local dimensions, tactical commanders often find themselves having to develop a local "strategy" or "theory of success" for their areas of operations. These should be expressed clearly in the commander's intent and overall concept.

The question of whether to seek a local military, political, or negotiated victory is a first-order issue. The theory of success may change over time as leaders gain information and make assessments. The good ones develop such a concept and then apply the appropriate methods (security, governance, economic support, communication) based on available means to achieve their ends. This also means that at higher tactical, operational, and strategic levels, commanders need to provide the right balance of guidance and freedom of action so local commanders can develop the approach best suited to their unique environments, while remaining within the proper boundaries.

Perhaps the most significant shortcoming recent counterinsurgencies have experienced has been the inability to turn initial gains into durable success.

An odd debate has developed whether a counterinsurgent should focus on killing or capturing the insurgent or on gaining the trust and support of the population—whether the effort should be enemy-centric or population-centric. The question mistakes tactics for strategy. The commander's concept, or theory of success, must drive the tactics, not the reverse. In most cases, commanders will need to find an appropriate balance.

A different way to consider the issue is through attrition and dislocation models. Attrition focuses on reducing the available capacity, the means, of the insurgents; dislocation aims to reduce the will of the insurgency and the population to support it. Both models are important, and both seek to affect cost-benefit calculations (more on this below), but in different ways.

Counterinsurgents typically default toward the attrition model. The aim of most efforts is to kill or capture existing insurgents and discourage others from joining through kinetic or non-kinetic means. Attrition works best when the insurgency is isolated from the population. When the insurgency enjoys active or passive popular support, however, insurgent numbers are generally elastic. The size of the insurgency tends to grow based on levels of counterinsurgent and government activity. Attrition-based counterinsurgency, in such cases, may lead to "fragile and reversible" gains but rarely to durable success. Such efforts may inflict spectacular flesh wounds on the insurgency, but generally fail to hit the jugular.

Dislocation-based counterinsurgency targets the will—the perceived need to generate and sustain insurgency in the first place. This approach is particularly critical when the insurgency enjoys popular support or acquiescence. The counterinsurgent, in this case, needs to understand the key drivers of instability and develop ways to affect cost-benefit calculations of various parties to redress those key drivers.

The essence of an offensive operation is to take from the enemy what he cannot afford to lose. In many cases, insurgents can afford to lose fighters, unit leaders, and weapons; these are flesh wounds. What insurgents generally cannot afford to lose is the active and passive support of the population. Dislocation is inherently offensive in nature, enabling the counterinsurgent to seize, retain, and exploit the initiative—to threaten the jugular.

Successful dislocation reduces the stakes for fighting—most salient issues are resolved through inclusive political (i.e., governance) processes. The hard-core ideologues or those who fight for personal gain grow increasingly isolated from the population; their aims are now at odds with those of the vast majority. Attrition can now be effective because the irreconcilable elements are unable to use the population to regenerate capacity. The jugular is now exposed.

Working both sides of the attrition and dislocation models at the right time, place, and manner is the art of counterinsurgency.

Understanding the cost-benefit calculations of key actors helps guide the ways and means by which counterinsurgents gain and maintain leverage. We need to understand the cost-benefit calculus from the perspectives of the various actors. Mirror-imaging will doom such efforts, creating significant perverse incentives and unintended consequences.

Learning and adaptation must be continuous. Understanding the environment and motivations and interests of key actors is part of learning. Counterinsurgents must also understand the effects of their actions on the environment; every action is likely to create a set of reactions or adaptations—some positive, some adverse.

The Boyd Cycle, or OODA Loop, can be adapted for counterinsurgency. The Observe (understand the environment) and Orient (determine critical threats, opportunities, and points of leverage) phases are the first part of learning. The Decision and Action phases are when we apply capabilities to generate change. The next Observe phase is when we assess the effects of our actions and determine the necessary adaptations (Orient).

Counterinsurgents must be on guard against the problem of being content with a single adaptation. The environment is not static. The other actors adapt as well. Their adaptations also generate change. If the counterinsurgent adapts only once, believing he has "broken the code," he will soon find his efforts increasingly ineffective, or even counterproductive.

In reality, there are many cycles of adaptation occurring in the environment. Each cycle affects other cycles. Context shifts and changes constantly, often in very subtle ways.

Each particular cycle of adaptation creates a new equilibrium and a new set of disruptions. These alter various challenges and opportunities. In the competitive and interactive nature of conflict, each actor in the environment seeks to address challenges and exploit opportunities—to alter the equilibrium in his favor.

The best counterinsurgents recognize the need for continuous learning and adaptation. They create an environment that encourages and demands it.

Much of what I described above is political, social, economic, and cultural in nature. This begs the question of whether such issues are the military's to deal with. Some argue that the military's job is to kill people and break things. Success in counterinsurgency, however, requires leaders to do more. The military's ultimate job is to fight and win the nation's wars and achieve national objectives. This book offers insight into how commanders can think through the challenges of doing so.

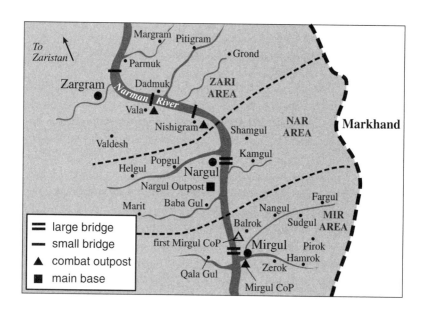

LIST OF CHARACTERS
AND GROUPS

NARABAD TRIBES AND ETHNIC GROUPS

Nar tribe: Primary tribe in the Nargul area. Rival of Mir tribe. Clans: Dust, Wani, Bog, Qala.

Mir tribe: Primary tribe in the Mirgul area. Rival of the Nar tribe. Clans: Khosi, Suk, Merk, Gork.

Zari tribe: Primary tribe in northwest Narabad. Prefer to be in Zaristan province. Different ethnicity from the Nar and Mir. Clans: Salar, Bamal, Zargot, Kala.

Marzin: Distinct ethnic group originating in Markhand. Primarily migrant farm workers. Have difficult relationships with Nar, Mir, and Zari. Clans: Hadu, Zug.

RELIGION

Jamdali: Primary religion in Khanastan

Domol: Radical school of Jamdali, practiced by Takriri insurgent groups

Hambali: Moderate school of Jamdali, practiced by most in Narabad and Khanastan

Jamma Rhun: School of Jamdali practiced by Zari tribe

INSURGENT GROUPS

Takriri: Primary insurgent group in Khanastan, follows Domol sect of Jamdali.

Zari-Sattar: Zari tribe insurgent group, led by Akhtar Gul in Archon and Markhand Wars, taken over by Sher Wali after Akhtar Gul's death.

GOVERNMENT OFFICIALS

Al'a Dust: Provincial chief of police

Bar Pak: Provincial governor

Lieutenant Colonel Naseem Hazam: Khanastan National Army battalion commander. Former insurgent leader in Markhand wars. From the Torag tribe of southern Khanastan.

NAR LEADERS

Afzal: Elder from Popgul.

Al'a Dust: Chief of police for Narabad province, cousin of Mo Dust. Important Nar tribe insurgent leader in Archon and Markhand wars. Blood feud with Bala Khan.

Mo Dust: Shura leader of Nar tribe. Dust clan.

MIR LEADERS

Bala Khan: Insurgent leader of Mir tribe during Archon and Markhand wars. Khosi clan. Blood feud with Al'a Dust.

Hamid Gul: Son of Saki Gul, subordinate leader to Bala Khan. Resides in Balrok.

Mir Hamza: Subordinate leader to Bala Khan. Resides in Qala Gul. Qala clan.

Saki Gul: Mir tribe elder, former teacher of Bala Khan. Has homes in Balrok and Mirgul.

ZARI LEADERS

Abdul Watan: Jamma Rhun cleric from Dadmuk. Bamal clan.

Akhtar Gul: Zari-Sattar insurgent leader during Archon and Markhand wars. Salar clan. Died under mysterious circumstances after Markhand war.

Akhtar Halim: Teacher from Parmuk. Bamal clan.

Ar Rahim: Shura leader of Zargram. Salar clan.

Ghani: Spokesman of Pitigram council. Bamal clan.

Mir Ali: Key Salar leader, brother of Akhtar Gul.

Sher Wali: Zari-Sattar insurgent leader from Pitigram. Bamal clan. Former subordinate of Akhtar Gul.

Zama: Leader of Zari hundred-man council. Salar clan.

INTRODUCTION

My battalion was alerted to deploy to Narabad Province in the Republic of Khanastan, a newly formed state that emerged from the collapse of Archon, a former Asian petty dictatorship that unraveled in a succession-of-power crisis. An insurgency had been ongoing for nearly two decades in the Khanastan region of the country, supported by neighboring Markhand and given funding by U.S. intelligence agencies.

Most of Archon was forcibly absorbed into Markhand, whose troops deployed there on the pretext of preventing instability from spilling over into its borders. Markhand had been a lukewarm ally of the United States; the latter's support was mainly an effort to balance the power of Archon and maintain friendly relations in the region. Several United Nations resolutions failed to stop the Markhand offensive.

A popular revolt was staged in the resource-rich region of Khanastan to prevent the Markhand conquest. After years of bloody fighting, the Markhand forces withdrew, and Khanastan declared its independence. It was immediately recognized by most countries, including the United States. A United Nations peacekeeping force was sent there to ensure stability. International sanctions were imposed upon Markhand.

A new coalition government emerged in Khanastan, formed primarily from the victorious armed factions.

Troubles emerged a couple years later, as various dissatisfied groups—many of whom were left out of the ruling coalition or excluded from the spoils of victory—began agitating for greater representation. An insurgency grew rapidly.

The primary insurgent group across the new country was the Takriri, named after their leader Takar Gul. There were other smaller groups, such as the Zari-Sattar in the Zari tribal area of Narabad, but the Takriri were considered the biggest threat.

Rumors abounded that Markhand was supporting the Takriri and other insurgent groups, and plenty of intelligence reports supported those assertions. Markhand flatly denied the allegations and claimed it wanted to become a strategic partner of the United States, despite the friction over its acquisition of former Archon territory.

The Takriri followed an extremist version of Jamdali, the primary religion in the area. It did not take our soldiers long to develop shorthand names for the enemy, referring to them as "Taks" or "Jammers."

As the Takriri-led insurgency grew more violent by 2025 and began targeting the U.N. peacekeeping mission, the United States and others decided to deploy military forces to bolster the effort. The new government of Khanastan was plagued by corruption and lack of capacity, problems that were exacerbated by the insurgency. The United States and others felt that Khanastan could become an important partner, and they had critical interests in gaining greater stability in a potentially volatile region.

We knew plenty about Archon, Khanastan, Markhand, and other states in the region, but very few had any firsthand experience on the ground there. After long wars in Afghanistan and Iraq and sustained economic problems, the United States and others had little appetite for further engagements for several years. As the economic crises subsided, and the memory of the long wars began to fade, America once again began playing a larger role in global affairs.

Still, the military had had little practice in counterinsurgency over the past decade, returning to its focus on conventional war. A feverish effort took place to dust off the old counterinsurgency manual and examine the lessons of Afghanistan and Iraq. Although Khanastan was very different in many ways, those wars would provide a decent point of entry into developing a framework for a new counterinsurgency effort.

Also rediscovered was a DARPA research project called Counterinsurgency Challenge that was completed and initially tested in 2014. Although too late to have any impact on the Afghanistan and Iraq wars—which had run their course by then—the research project was kept alive by a small group of innovative thinkers who believed it would be useful again once America emerged from isolationism and reengaged in world affairs. By 2005, the country had done so.

Counterinsurgency Challenge was a virtual reality program modeled as a complex adaptive system. It was designed to simulate dynamically complex conflict situations, which some called "wicked" problems. Historical, political, economic, social, cultural, religious, and international factors, among many others, served as inputs to the program.

The program suffered great, and justified, criticism initially. In its early stages, it was unable to adequately model the complex human and structural interactions necessary to be worthwhile as a simulation. Improvements in mind-mapping and virtual reality technologies rectified most of these problems to the point that Counterinsurgency Challenge was a useful, albeit imperfect, tool. When combined with expertise of those with on-the-ground counterinsurgency experience to serve as mentors, it could assist the military in developing valuable mental models for future operations.

What makes the program so interesting was the "free-play" component. Significant advances in virtual intelligence enabled the cyber-characters in the program—villagers, insurgents, and my own "soldiers"—to exercise virtual "free will" in their decisions and actions. They did not rely upon a human player, with associated biases, to control them. They operated on their own volition using decision-making rules. The characters in the simulation also "learned" based on relative values programmed into the system. Actions that delivered outcomes deemed good got positive reinforcement in the learning system; negative feedback led to a reduction of behaviors that lead to bad outcomes. Built-in "pairwise comparisons"—the comparison of relative good between variables—enabled the characters to optimize choices.

A limiting factor of previous simulations was the fact that the "experts" had significant insight, if not direct control, of what the opposing forces were doing. This gave them a degree of omniscience that biased their coaching and lent artificiality to the mentoring. With Counterinsurgency Challenge, the mentors would have no more understanding than I would—the future and the outcomes of my decisions were of equal mystery and unpredictability.

Of course, the "experts" did not agree on everything—and some had quite opposing viewpoints—so I would have to sort through their advice as well as my own lessons as I prepared myself and my unit for the mission.

I spent a good deal of time learning about Narabad and Khanastan on my own. What follows is a brief synopsis.

Narabad was a mountainous area of Khanastan bordering on Markhand. The highly diverse and poorly educated population consisted of various ethnic groups and tribes and their clans. The social structures had eroded over the years, and strife was common between and among them.

Local governance councils operated on social consensus for decision making. The official government was designed to mediate disputes and play the role of honest broker. Corruption and incompetence, however, undermined this system. Community councils stopped meeting in conflict-ridden areas. Although people yearned for the days of the councils, the credibility of the traditional system had eroded. Local strongmen ruled by intimidation. Some supported the insurgency, others supported the government. Strongmen on all sides profited from the conflict.

Although rich in timber, gems, and minerals, the country had an economic potential that remained untapped outside of a robust black market. The people, with the exception of the local power brokers and their networks, were poor. Unemployment was high; literacy rates were low, even more so for women.

Insurgent activity in the area was significant, bordering on insurrection in some locations. Various local insurgent leaders allied with one another and received training, resources, command and control, and financing from the senior leaders. Most of the population, it seemed, provided either active or passive support to the insurgent groups.

The dominant insurgent group was the Takriri, which was founded on an extreme religious ideology. The Takriri wanted to purify Khanastan by imposing their own social norms on the people. Khanastan did not have a history of religious extremism and most people rejected the Takriri ideology, but the insurgency gained significant support due to popular dissatisfaction with the government and its rampant corruption and abuse of power. The Takriri grew adept at listening to the people and taking action to support them—in marked contrast to the government.

The Zari-Sattar was the other main insurgent group in the Narabad area, supported mainly by the Zari, an ethnic group living in the mountainous northeast of Khanastan. The group, led by the charismatic Akhtar Gul, enjoyed wide popular support among the tribe during the Markhand wars. The Zari-Sattar wanted autonomy for their people. After Akhtar Gul's death, a faction of the group was taken over by a religious zealot named Sher Wali.

Jamdali was the primary religion in Khanastan. It was a monotheistic religion with a strong degree of mysticism in several of its sects. The dominant sect in Khanastan was the Hambali. The Takriri followed the Domol orthodoxy, while the Zari-Sattar and most of the Zari people followed the Jamma Rhun school.

The society was patriarchal. Men participated in local politics and made the official decisions. Women, however, played highly influential roles behind the scenes.

Malign influence from Markhand exacerbated instability. Markhand was suffering from its own insurgency in the border areas. Insurgents and militants could draw upon a vast supply of arms, ammunition, and expertise from across the border. The people of Narabad tended to blame their problems on Markhand, as did the Khanastan government.

My battalion was colocated with the Khanastan National Army (KNA) Battalion, which was commanded by Lieutenant Colonel Naseem Hazam. He was a powerful, rather heavyset former insurgent leader from the Torag tribe of southern Khanastan. His black hair and full beard framed rich brown eyes that immediately made you feel comfortable in his presence.

The provincial governor was a man named Bar Pak, a fat, unkempt-looking businessman and politician from a different area of Khanastan. As with all provincial governors in Khanastan, he was appointed by the central government. The chief of police was a former local insurgent leader named Al'a Dust. He lived in Nargul but also had a house in Baba Gul.

These factors and many more were programmed into the simulation. With this brief understanding, I was placed in the Counterinsurgency Challenge virtual reality simulator.

I had two mentors, Mick Lundy, a former commander and mentor of mine, and Alexander Cross, who I only knew by reputation as a highly intelligent retired officer who later worked at senior levels in the defense department.

The first mentor, Mick Lundy, asked me about my mission. I replied that it was to defeat the insurgency. "Good," said the second mentor, Alexander Cross, "but what exactly does that mean?"

"I have to eliminate the insurgency in Narabad—kill them, capture them, drive them out of the area."

"Okay," said Mick, "you're on the right track. Let's go kill some Jammers."

Alexander looked at me quizzically. "Good luck with that," he said, as I donned the virtual reality device and entered the simulation.

A Dose of (Virtual) Reality

I had been in simulations before, but nothing quite this realistic. I was struck by the vastness of the terrain. Sharp pine- and snow-covered mountains reached over ten thousand feet toward the heavens. Steep, glacier-cut valleys contained rapidly flowing streams and rivers whose current would carry an object several miles in under an hour. Narrow plains on either side of the major rivers formed the arable land. Terraces were cut into the mountainsides to increase plots suitable for cultivation. Underwater springs and aquifers irrigated the land and provided fresh water for the people.

The major towns were located along the rivers. Smaller villages developed in the mountain valleys. Over time, the "have-nots," seeking land and autonomy, had moved out of the major villages and deeper in the mountains. Arable land and water were precious resources and matters of survival. Feuds emerged routinely between villages and within them over control and access to land and water. With little economy outside the black market, people in these valleys had to farm to live. Since arable land was scarce in these valleys, farmers had little surplus crops for trade. A seminomadic group, the Marzin, tended the fields and livestock for the wealthier landowners. The generally suitable arrangement was interrupted every few years by expulsion and fighting when the Marzin were perceived to be "squatting" on a plot of land for too long.

The men dressed in traditional robes and garments; the wealthier ones were identified by the quality of their shoes. Women wore brightly colored dresses. The people were quite pleasant, often amicable. They had a great sense of humor, developed over generations as an emotional outlet in response to persistent conflict and hard living. After so many years of strife, they were cautious about revealing any information. They understood little about our society; theirs was opaque to us.

They became masters of "social intelligence." They were expert at picking up the nuances of facial expressions, body language, and tone of voice. For them, it was a matter of survival. We had volumes of information—a lot of explicit data. How all of that data connected, what it all meant, and how it affected relationships and points of view were elusive to us. The implicit knowledge—the connection of it all—was intuitive to them. They half expected us to know it; we rarely even knew the questions to ask to begin to understand.

Most people spoke Khandu, but various ethnic groups had local dialects as well. We had to use interpreters to communicate with them. Some of the interpreters were better than others; a few were downright dangerous in their lack of practical English. Because a local dialect was the most common vernacular for some of the more remote groups, Khandu was often a second language. Sometimes a statement from one person had to be translated by another into Khandu, and then translated by the interpreter into English.

Initial Assessment at Nargul Base

The Forward Operating Base (FOB) that housed the battalion was a sprawling complex in flatlands along the west side of the river. The base was roughly five kilometers south of the town of Nargul, which was on the west side of the Narman River. Mirgul was located thirty kilometers south on the east side of the river. The former was the provincial capital, a collection of densely packed wood, mud, and stone buildings along narrow, congested, trash-ridden streets. The wealthier places were easily identified by the presence of trash. The poor families could not afford it.

The KNA battalion colocated with me was poorly trained and equipped. The commander, Naseem Hazam, seemed to be a good leader who cared about his men and was making the best of a difficult situation. Naseem was a highly respected insurgent leader in the Markhand wars.

The Nar were the primary tribe of the province; the Mir were their rivals. Both tribes had intermarried over time, so the villages were intermixed. Nonetheless, Nargul was much wealthier than Mirgul, and Mir people in Nargul identified more with the people in that town than with their kinsmen in Mirgul. Still, infighting occurred in both.

I was approached by the provincial governor, Bar Pak, and a group of men he identified as the provincial council. They came to welcome me and my unit and discuss the problems in the area. I was delighted by the meeting and comforted that the governor spoke fairly decent English, had spent some time in the U.S. and Western Europe, and had a provincial council to represent the people.

Our discussion was very friendly and informative. The governor said the people were poor and needed a lot of projects and economic support. He complained bitterly of the interference from Markhand. Militant leaders in that country fomented violence in the area and paid people to fight. They had gained various allies in the province.

"We must stop the bad people from Markhand!" he shouted as he pounded his first on the table. "We will never have peace in Narabad until the problem over there is solved." I asked for his advice on how to handle the problem. He said we should focus on the border area—prevent the insurgents from crossing into Narabad—and punish those who are serving as their puppets here.

I took all of this advice to heart. My mind began racing about how to secure the border in such terrain. The enemy was known to move unarmed and dispersed, like ordinary groups of civilians, to avoid detection by our surveillance systems. They placed weapons caches throughout the area to arm themselves. They used villages along the "rat lines" as "lily pads" to rest, refit, plan, and hide.

Ominous references by some of the provincial council members alerted me to Mirgul and other villages that dotted the map near the Markhand border. "The Takriri are strong there," they told me.

We were attacked repeatedly by rockets from the mountains south and east of the river in the Mirgul area. Our patrols along the main river roads would get ambushed on occasion, mainly sporadic fire. We encountered some mines and "improvised explosive devices" (IEDs), but nothing alarming. I needed to take the fight to the enemy before the pressure got worse.

I met with Naseem afterward to tell him about the meeting and my concerns about Mirgul. "Not everything here is as it seems," Naseem counseled. "We should try to communicate with the people there first to determine their grievances and problems."

The problem, I thought to myself, was that the people were insurgents and were shooting at us. Get rid of the insurgents, and the problem would be solved. I began to wonder about Naseem's commitment to the fight. I would need to watch him closely.

I focused surveillance assets on the border and conducted several missions to interdict rat lines into Narabad. Most of the missions were "dry holes," meaning there was no enemy activity. We did kill a few insurgents in these missions, but attacks on the FOB persisted. I lost two of my virtual soldiers to an IED explosion a few kilometers north of the Mirgul bridge.

I was beginning to understand where the problem was concentrated.

Even in the virtual world, I was incensed at the death of my men. The reality of it all gave the experience an emotional component I had never anticipated. I had never felt bloodlust before, but now the single-minded need for revenge pulsed through my veins. If this was not bloodlust, then it was awfully close.

A few days after the IED incident, I met once again with Governor Bar Pak and the council. They expressed their condolences at the loss of my soldiers. They reiterated their observation about the bad people in Markhand working together with allies in Narabad to create instability. "You know where the problems are," said Bar Pak. "These people need to be punished. They are supporting the Takriri against the government. You have to set examples to be successful here. People respect force." The provincial chief of police, Al'a Dust, nodded slowly in agreement.

Council member Mo Dust, one of the graybeards from Nargul, agreed but also counseled, "Those who are friendly also need to be rewarded. You have to strike the right balance. We are poor people. Give aid and projects and economic support to the ones who cooperate. Concentrate your force in punishing the ones fighting. Then you set an example of the benefits of cooperation and the consequences of fighting." The other members of the council were in agreement.

Their advice made a lot of sense to me. Reward and punishment were concepts that cut across cultural lines. Soon we began working together with the governor on aid and economic support to the areas he suggested. We sent more patrols and surveillance to the south of the FOB, toward Mirgul and surrounding villages.

Naseem still insisted that we should try to talk to the people. He just did not seem to get it . . . and this was his country. He began making up reasons why his soldiers could not go on patrols with us. He was becoming worse than useless. Frustrated, I decided to go it alone—we needed to get after the enemy. I let my brigade commander know about Naseem's unwillingness to fight and the need for him to be replaced with someone who had the right mindset.

Taking the Fight to Mirgul

Enemy contract increased. We were taking the fight to new areas. We needed to contest this enemy safe haven. We killed a lot of insurgents. The more we probed into these areas, the more contact we had. And the more it became clear that Mirgul was the center of instability, and that insurgent leaders were spreading their influence in the area.

I needed to get more fidelity on the insurgency in Mirgul. I had various reports on different leaders, but everything was pretty sketchy in the first few weeks. We finally got a break when Chief of Police Al'a Dust said he had a source in Mirgul.

He brought the source to the FOB one evening. We had worked out a protocol to bring him in secretly. He explained that Bala Khan was the man responsible for the insurgent attacks. He was a Takriri insurgent leader and had long been in the pocket of Markhand. He was trying to take control of the province. He planned attacks, financed and resourced fighters, and fomented anger against the government.

The source explained that Bala Khan intended to mount a large-scale attack against our forces. The rockets, probes, and ambushes had allowed them to understand our procedures. He had seen enough to be confident in success. The source also hinted that Bala Khan had some support on the inside, meaning some of the day workers on the FOB.

I took notes with great interest. Al'a Dust told me that while it was unwise to put too much faith in a single report, what the source said was consistent with what others had told him. He would continue working to get more information.

Al'a Dust was a famous and highly regarded former militia leader in Narabad. During the insurrection against Markhand, he repeatedly ambushed and defeated Markhand forces. He was a large man, just over six feet tall. His face bore the scars of war, including a raised line across his right cheek toward his ear marking the graze of a bullet. He walked with a limp—his foot was nearly blown off in an assassination attempt during the Markhand war. The reduction in physical activity from the injury was not matched by a corresponding reduction in caloric intake, however; he had grown fat though not yet obese. The fire in his yellow eyes left no doubt of his ferocity.

I heard various allegations of his brutality against those who supported Markhand. I did not know how credible those allegations were; they came to me early in our time from people who appeared to be personal enemies of his. While I did not doubt Al'a Dust was capable of brutality, he had shown himself time and again to be a reliable partner and tough commander.

I would continue to hold him and his forces to standards of proper conduct. He dealt swiftly with incompetence and policemen who we caught abusing power with the people. He took such reports seriously, perhaps because of allegations over his past. Overall, I was glad Dust was on our side.

Naseem was another matter. He asked what I knew about the background of the people giving reports to us, saying that people give information on others for many different reasons. I said that I was a soldier, not a social scientist or psychiatrist. Their issues did not matter to me— the information did. He walked off . . . just looking for another excuse to not fight.

Over the course of the next few weeks, contact with the enemy grew more intense. I was amazed at how many insurgents we killed. We must have destroyed several networks already, which had to put a dent in their operations over time. By our count, the enemy should have only a couple of local cells left.

Two more of my virtual soldiers were killed and several wounded. Still, the "exchange rate," a Mick Lundy term for friendly versus enemy casualty ratios, was dramatically in our favor. We were kicking the enemy's ass and the enemy knew it. The insurgent leaders reportedly had to bring in fighters from Markhand to supplement their ranks. We were breaking them.

We had a few more sources come in to corroborate the reports against Bala Khan. The fact that some of the sources were from Mirgul indicated to me that the people were turning against him and that our balanced approach was working. Support the cooperative with aid and development; take the militants to the woodshed. People would soon realize the benefits of working with us and the price of being against us—they would ultimately choose self-interest. I did not care if they liked us. I wanted them to respect us and their government and give up the fight.

Two of the sources we considered most reliable each reported that Bala Khan would have a meeting at his home on the east side of Mirgul in three days. Hundreds of fighters would attend to make final preparations for an attack on our outpost. Bala Khan was getting desperate—he had to gain a tactical success quickly or risk the disillusionment of his supporters and their potential defection to the government. This was a last-ditch gamble. He did not know we were on to him and ready to ruin his day.

We began planning for what would be the final showdown in the province. We would catch Bala Khan in the act and annihilate his forces when they foolishly gathered at his home. He must be truly losing his mind to attempt such a brazen and risky move.

Two other sources gave pretty much the same story a day later. Al'a Dust, Bar Pak, and I coordinated a general plan; my staff worked feverishly to iron out the details.

Naseem sat on his ass, refusing to participate. I was glad; I could not afford wasting any more time or command calories on him.

I wondered what had happened to him—a tough insurgent commander turned soft. Maybe he had simply seen too much.

I asked him once about the tattoo he wore on his left arm.

"It represents four letters in my language. What they stand for is very dear to me. Maybe one day I will tell you about them."

I also asked him about the Markhand wars.

Naseem's gaze grew distant. "Those were terrible times." He shuddered. "There are not words in my language or yours that can describe the horror that people can do to one another. My wife and children were murdered."

"That must have been very difficult for you," I said.

"The images may fade over time," he replied, "but they never leave. Those who have seen such horrors are no longer as eager to kill—unless they are crazy. I hope you have never experienced such things."

"I have not," I replied, wondering whether there was some hidden criticism in his answer.

The virtual war was interrupted at this point by my mentor Mick Lundy, who was an absolute expert on tactical operations. Mick was a warrior. A hard-bitten, physically fit man who talked soldier talk. An articulate killer, people said. He was a smart, brave, no-nonsense kind of soldier. His superiors loved him for his combat mentality. His soldiers differed in their opinions. Some believed he put their lives on the line for personal glory, but others would follow him to the ends of the earth.

He talked me through weapons-effects, angles of fire, primary and alternate HLZs (Helicraft Landing Zones), support-by-fire, attack-by-fire, assault force positions, and directions of attack. I learned more about light infantry mountain combat tactics in that thirty-minute tutorial than in eighteen years in the infantry. He was as excited as I was about the attack. He did recommend that I get some KNA on the mission, despite Naseem's uselessness, to put a "Khanastan face" on the operation.

Assault on Mirgul

I reentered the simulation.

We had surveillance drones overhead, flying high enough to make no perceptible noise twenty thousand feet below. Strike aircraft waited several miles out. My quick reaction force and assault aircraft were assembled to conduct site exploitation after the airstrikes.

I asked Naseem for some KNA—ten of them would be enough. He said that he doubted the necessity of the mission and that his soldiers needed to be employed as a unit, a platoon at a minimum. He offered to lead it himself. This was just another excuse for inaction. He knew that transport aircraft was scarce and that I could not afford to replace a platoon of my soldiers with his poorly trained KNA on such a mission. I told him not to bother.

I still had my doubts Bala Khan would be as reckless as the reports indicated. Those were dispelled as groups of people, generally five to ten at a time, began moving toward his house, their normal technique for massing forces. Several were clearly armed with rifles; others carried large bundles, most likely ammunition and other explosives.

Within about ninety minutes, the various groups congregated at the large, two-story compound that served as Bala Khan's lair. Clearly wealthy, Bala Khan had constructed guard towers at the corners of the outer walls of the complex. The spacious inner courtyard had various gardens, a small orchard, and large gathering places for guests. It was bursting with militants.

Given the guard towers and the number of fighters in the compound, a direct assault would be costly. The best option was an airstrike to kill or wound most of the fighters, followed by the air assault to exploit the target and round up the rest of the militants. Hopefully, Bala Khan would be among the captured so we could gain more information on his contacts in Markhand. I would also prefer he not be a martyr to the cause.

The potential for civilian casualties weighed on me. While I had no sympathy for those who supported Bala Khan and his fighters—and everyone there clearly did—I did not wish to see otherwise innocent people killed. I talked to the JAG officer—the lawyer—ahead of time, who assured me it was a valid military target. We did a collateral damage estimate and adjusted the munitions accordingly to limit our weapons' effects on adjacent homes. My chain of command approved; the brigade commander was really excited about the upcoming decisive action.

I was confident that we would destroy Bala Khan's compound and that the damage to surrounding homes would be insignificant, minus some blown-out windows. We would pay compensation as required. I was confident we had done everything we could to limit potential harm.

"This ends now!" I said as I ordered weapons release. Everyone in the "Situational Awareness Room" was transfixed to the screen. The two-second time delay between the strike aircraft video feed and the drone feed gave a "replay" effect that would enable us to see the strike twice.

Four five-hundred-pound laser-guided munitions would soon descend toward their targets. I added four concrete munitions to take out each guard tower. The concrete bomb would merely destroy the towers, but would not explode or send shrapnel toward adjacent houses.

The assault force circled five miles from the target area, just as Mick had suggested.

"Thirty seconds to weapon release!" announced the JTAC. I was glued to the screen.

"Weapon release! Two minutes to impact!" Four laser-guided bombs and four laser-guided concrete canisters raced to their aim points.

"One minute to impact!"

"Thirty seconds!"

"The Jammers have no idea what is about to hit them," said my operations officer.

After what seemed an eternity, the bombs detonated precisely on target. I half-imagined I saw an armed militant looking up a second before impact, as if he heard the whistle of the incoming bombs. A cloud of smoke and flash billowed from the compound.

The assault force was inbound just as the weapons impacted. Five minutes was plenty of time for us to assess the situation, observe for secondary explosions, and ensure we could adjust to an alternate landing zone if necessary. It was also close enough to impact to prevent the enemy from recovering from the shock of the airstrike.

The force landed in two positions: One landed east of the compound to establish a support-by-fire position and take down any "squirters" in that direction; the assault force was inserted to the north and began to make its way toward the rubbled compound.

"Perfect," I heard Mick Lundy whisper from the background.

Fire began to erupt from adjacent compounds. "Those bastards!" I shouted as we saw through the UAV feed two men in the assault force go down to enemy fire. A squad from the assault platoon peeled off in textbook fashion to lay suppressive fire on the compounds while the remainder drove on to the objective.

The firefight grew more intense. It seemed like the whole village erupted. One squad from the assault platoon was pinned down; the rest of the platoon was now engaged in a firefight with other compounds that had joined in the fight. The support-by-fire position was raking the enemy with machine-gun fire, but the rounds failed to penetrate the sturdy walls.

The support force fired a Javelin—an antitank missile that had proven to be a great bunker-buster—into a compound. The fire subsided momentarily but erupted again with renewed fury.

We were still two hundred meters from the objective and going nowhere fast. We had three soldiers killed and six wounded, two critically. Now I had a medical evacuation emergency on a red-hot landing zone. The assault force was rapidly becoming combat ineffective.

With the forces pinned down and unable to reposition, I ordered airstrikes on the closest compounds. Five two-thousand-pound bombs homed in on their targets and detonated nearly simultaneously on the compounds. That eliminated the main sources of fire.

The medical evacuation helicopters swept in while the jets conducted "show-of-force" missions—low-level passes near the objective area. With the casualties extracted, I directed the assault aircraft to recover the force on the ground and return to base. The gain from the mission was no longer worth the cost—the two critically wounded died. We would find out whether we got Bala Khan, and how many of his fighters, soon enough.

We saw very little insurgent movement around the target area and adjacent compounds. We must have killed or seriously wounded over a hundred fighters. That should eliminate the threat from Bala Khan for good. The cost to our force was high, but we risked losing far more over time had we not conducted the mission.

Aftermath: Nargul Base

The next day, Al'a Dust and Bar Pak visited to tell me that Bala Khan had somehow escaped but scores of his fighters and others had been killed. The Mirgul insurgents had been delivered a devastating, perhaps fatal, blow. Maybe Bala Khan would sue for peace.

An eerie silence came over the village. We watched from the UAV feed a few people wandering around burying the dead. No one else came out of their compounds.

We began getting media reports about a massive number of civilian casualties in Mirgul. The Khanastan president was condemning the raid, claiming that two hundred innocent civilians had been killed. Bar Pak was interviewed by a local station—he had turned on me too, claiming outrage over the "reckless disregard for civilian lives."

Unbelievable! Bar Pak and Al'a Dust had supported, even encouraged, the raid all along. Now that fat bastard was blaming *me* and calling me a war criminal. Five of my soldiers were dead and four wounded in a huge firefight that had eliminated the key threat in the province, and they were condemning *me* for taking the fight to the enemy!

A group of Mir elders from Nargul, whose relatives lived in Mirgul, came to the FOB and requested to see me. One of the "sources" was among them. I was pretty worked up by this time and in no mood for people to tell me we killed civilians when I could see for myself that they were a bunch of insurgents. I grabbed the first interpreter I could find.

"Commander," one of the elders began, "we are very distressed by such terrible losses."

"Thank you for your condolences; they were good soldiers."

The elder looked at me curiously; others began to fidget. "I do not care about those people," he said. "This must stop."

"I agree, and I think it will now that the criminals are dead."

"Yes, criminals, that is what we call people who kill the innocent."

"I can kill more of them if you tell me where they are," I replied matter-of-factly.

The elder appeared puzzled; the interpreter was clearly not one of the best. The others began rubbing their faces and pulling at their beards.

"I do not understand," he said curtly but politely.

"TELL. ME. WHERE. THEY. ARE. SO. I. CAN. KILL. THEM. FOR. YOU." I said deliberately. I hated these meetings and was rapidly losing patience.

"I understand. We must go . . . You will hear from us soon."

I thanked him for his support as he walked out of the room with the group. I reported the encounter to the brigade commander and let him know that the elders from Nargul had expressed their condolences for our soldiers and that they agreed criminals were killed. I was confident they would be back to provide more information on any remaining insurgents.

Situation in Nargul

A few days later there was a deadly IED strike between the base and Nargul—the first time this had happened. Four soldiers were killed in a massive explosion. Al'a Dust, whom I had not seen since the operation, told me the insurgents were seeking revenge and were now harassing the people in Nargul.

I sent a patrol to Nargul to find out what was happening. Two soldiers were killed as they entered the market, shot by marksmen on the rooftops. A firefight erupted as my soldiers returned fire and formed a perimeter—trying to protect themselves as well as the remaining people in the nearly deserted market. One of the people inside the perimeter detonated a suicide bomb, killing four more soldiers and injuring seven others.

I launched the quick reaction force by ground assault to the scene. The patrol struck an IED on the outskirts of the village, which killed all five in the lead vehicle. The patrol proceeded on foot, leaving a squad to guard the vehicles, and eventually made link-up with the force in Nargul. After about twelve hours, we extracted everyone back to the FOB. Several people from the village came out to help. We treated about twenty civilians who had been wounded by shrapnel from the suicide bombing or had gotten caught in the crossfire. I was surprised that insurgents had been able to come into the village undetected and carry off such an attack.

My soldiers began to develop an intense hatred for the "Jammers."

Two of my companies had taken significant losses by this time. Three soldiers committed suicide over the next three weeks, and several more were displaying serious signs of combat stress. Morale plummeted as attacks on the FOB and our patrols continued to increase. A ring of IEDs surrounded the base and made patrolling even more difficult. Bar Pak and Al'a Dust narrowly escaped assassination; Nargul experienced bloody "green-on-green" (civilian-on-civilian) fighting. The province was quickly descending into chaos.

"This game is bullshit!" I heard Mick Lundy exclaim as I came out of the simulator. "Your tactics were perfect. This is completely ridiculous."

"Surely you have seen things get weird in combat, Mick." Alexander Cross had come down to the simulator to discuss the event.

Mick shook his head. "I have seen some of these things happen, but not in combination like this."

I had to agree. I had done everything by the book, and my tactics were perfect, just like Mick had taught me many years before. There had to be a glitch in the system.

I looked at the clock. To my surprise, I had only been in the simulator for few hours. How the program could enable you to experience such a vast expanse of time so quickly was extraordinary. Four months of combat had unfolded in just four hours.

Although the scenario outcome seemed really far-fetched to me, I was curious about what had happened. There was no controller of the game—within the virtual reality each individual had artificial intelligence and free will. Mick and Alex had no idea beforehand what the outcome would be, and they had no more insight than I did at this point of why the individuals in the game made the decisions they did. They lived the scenario through my eyes only. The program was so complex that even with today's computing power, it would take the techs several hours to sort through it all to determine why things happened the way they did.

Initial Debrief

"Tell us what you experienced," began Alex.

I recounted the scenario and my key decisions: the coordination with the governor and police chief, the assessment that the insurgency led by Bala Khan was concentrated in Mirgul, the intelligence gathering and verification, the operation in Mirgul to destroy Bala Khan's network. I also explained my frustration with Naseem.

"Everything was going well up to that point. Even the operation, despite the loss of five soldiers, was a success by any measure—we killed over a hundred insurgents. Even though Bala Khan lived, it would take a very, very long time for him to regenerate that kind of combat power.

"Then things began to go wrong. Naseem refused to conduct any further operations. The governor and police chief betrayed me, but the elders still seemed supportive. Then we had the fight in Nargul, the suicide bombing, the IED belts. Bala Khan must have been able to recruit scores of fighters from Markhand—there is no way any local fighters were left. We must have killed off a generation of young men in that area.

"Still, that doesn't explain why the friendly locals in Nargul didn't report the IEDs the influx of insurgents from Markhand. Nargul isn't that big; they must have known foreigners were there. It doesn't make sense."

"A glitch in the system," said Mick. "I like the program, but there are obviously some flaws to work out. Still, we have plenty of lessons we can learn from this. Let's talk about your tactics."

Mick and I reviewed each plan and engagement, down to the fine, technical details. Alex listened in but was preoccupied with other thoughts. Maybe he just wasn't as good a tactician. Mick gave a clinic in urban tactics, while I took notes furiously so I could improve my performance in the next fight.

Still, we both agreed that my tactics were superb. There was no way, especially after killing so many insurgents, that violence could have increased to such intensity—especially in Nargul, where I had poured in so much money and support. But even if the game was flawed, it had generated an intense tactical discussion with Mick, which alone made the experience worthwhile.

"Tell me about the population," inquired Alex, as he looked up from his notebook. I had heard that he talked about the importance of the people in counterinsurgency. I thought it was fundamentally flawed because it focused on the wrong side of the equation. We're soldiers, not social workers.

I recounted that there were a few different ethnic groups and tribes, that they feuded with one another, and all seemed to want money—pretty normal stuff.

"Was the insurgency supported by any particular group?"

"Well, Bala Khan was a Tak leader from the Mir tribe. Most of the people of Mirgul and the surrounding valleys were from the same tribe. Nargul had a mix, with the Mir as a minority group. Most of the Nar tribe seemed to be with the government. Markhand was the big supporter of the insurgency. I probably should have focused even more on border interdiction after the Bala Khan mission—and probably should have anticipated that they would go after Nargul to undermine our efforts and take the attention away from Mirgul."

"What is the nature of the conflict? Why do you think the people were fighting?"

"Because they're insurgents!" Mick was being playful, but I sensed a note of sarcasm.

I didn't have a good answer to those questions. I never really thought about the "nature of the conflict" other than that this was an insurgency that we were fighting. To me that was good enough, but Alex seemed to be trying to get at something else.

"As to why people were fighting," I said, "well, that's what insurgents do. Bala Khan was an insurgent leader, and some of the Mir people supported him. He got most of his support from Markhand. We needed to defeat him and his fighters to stabilize Narabad. The sanctuary across the border was a big problem."

"I was struck by the fact that the insurgency got more intense, and more widespread, after the Bala Khan mission," Alex observed. "What are your thoughts on that?"

"My assessment was that Bala Khan was able to recruit more fighters from Markhand."

"So what do you make of the fact that the violence seemed high over some periods of time and nearly nonexistent in others?"

I had not thought about that. I guessed it had something to do with a planning, resourcing, fighting cycle. Violence during the planning and logistical resupply periods would be low, followed by a period of fighting until supplies ran out, and then another planning and resupply cycle would begin.

"How about the governor and police chief and KNA commander; what was your assessment?"

"Naseem was worthless; he'd probably seen too many firefights. The governor and police chief were good, even though I could not quite explain their betrayal. The police chief was a local hero and fierce fighter. The governor was friendly and smart. He spoke good English. He certainly squeezed a lot of money out of me for projects to support his people."

"How did those projects come out? Who benefitted?"

This was also not something I had put many mental calories toward. The civil affairs team managed the details. I set the priority areas and which ones were cut off for being nonsupportive.

"Tell me about your impression of the conversation with the elders after the strike on Bala Khan."

"It was pretty straightforward. They came to express their condolences for our fallen heroes. They said they were tired of the criminals who killed innocents, and that I would hear from them soon. They were supposed to tell me about where more insurgents were located."

"Did you hear back from them?"

"No, I didn't—but that was about the time fighting erupted in Nargul. They must have gotten intimidated by the influx of insurgents from Markhand."

"What sort of contact did you have with the people in Mirgul? Were you able to build any relationships with them? Did you have a good feel for what was happening in the town and surrounding villages?"

"We really had no contact with the people in Mirgul, and I have way too much to worry about to waste time chitchatting with locals. I can see doing so with the governor and police chief—they need to handle the people. We got most of our information about Mirgul from source reporting, which seems to have been very reliable."

"Very interesting. There are some gaps in our knowledge to think through, and maybe a few assumptions worth questioning. We will learn more when we get the report. Excellent tactics, by the way."

I could not tell if that last comment was a backhanded compliment or not, but Alex seemed to see things very differently from the way Mick and I did. The outcome made little sense to me or to Mick. Alex seemed less surprised. I looked forward to a good night's sleep and the readout tomorrow morning.

Feedback Session

The techs were poring over the data all night. Alex made them check the logic and feedback loops in the program twice to determine whether the system had malfunctioned in any way. He knew that would be the first question from me and Mick.

"All of the program parameters checked out," said Alex. "The explanation is interesting and may provide some food for thought."

The techs summarized the outcome of the scenario:

Bala Khan is a leader of the Mir tribe from Mirgul. He grew opposed to the Narabad government, even though he initially supported the formation of Khanastan. He has a long-standing feud with Al'a Dust, who is from the Nar tribe. The Mir and the Nar tribes feud with one another, and the Mir, who feel the government is against them, have turned to the Takriri.

Bala Khan had provided passive support to insurgents—he would not give them resources, nor would he encourage people to join the insurgency, but he did not hold them back either. He grew to believe that your forces were on the side of the Nar and the government in their dispute with the Mir.

On the night of the strike on his compound, Bala Khan was celebrating the wedding of his daughter. The gathering at his home was a party, attended by over one hundred people. Many were carrying guns for the celebratory gunfire after the vows were exchanged. The air strike killed most of his relatives. He escaped miraculously. The gunfire from the village during the air assault was from people who believed their village was under attack.

As a result of the strike, Bala Khan declared war on the foreign forces and sought assistance from the Takriri. Most of the Mir tribe joined immediately. Mir elders from Nargul came to the FOB to seek an explanation. They came away believing you were at war with the Mir tribe and had deliberately killed innocent civilians—their relatives. They decided to join the insurgency.

Nargul became violent, with infighting between the Nar and Mir. The Mir were convinced that the Nar instigated the airstrike. The IED belts were meant to keep you away from the villages. The suicide bomber was the groom from the wedding—his new wife had been killed in the airstrike.

Mick still insisted the outcome was far-fetched, but the narrative summary was a shock. The thought that Bar Pak and Al'a Dust had manufactured evidence against Bala Khan, and that their evidence had led me to order a strike that killed dozens of civilians, was unsettling. And the ramifications were extraordinary, both to my own force and to the mission.

"What did you learn from this?" asked Alex.

"I learned that I needed to know more about the situation before acting on reports. Bala Khan certainly was not a 'good guy,' but he was not an insurgent leader either—until I turned him into one. I knew that the Nar and Mir had some long-standing disputes but did not anticipate that I would be used by one group—especially by government officials—to strike at the other.

"But how," I asked, "after we killed so many fighters, did the enemy keep fighting? How much support did they get from Markhand?"

"According to the readout," replied Alex, "the vast majority of the fighters were locals. They received some resources, supplies, and trainers from Markhand, but the manpower support was negligible."

This didn't make any sense—we killed so many! The threat analysis said there were about five cells in the Mirgul area with about fifteen to twenty fighters each. I figured with the beating we gave them, all of those networks were eliminated.

"Welcome to COIN math!" Alex exclaimed.

"What?"

"COIN math—counterinsurgency math. If you have ten insurgents and you kill two, you are not necessarily left with eight. You might end up with more insurgents than the original ten, especially if civilian casualties were involved."

Mick was beside himself. "Now you're reinventing math? What kind of nonsense is this?"

"You tell me," intoned Alex calmly. "How many people live in Mirgul and the surrounding communities?"

"About seventy thousand to eighty thousand people, if I recall correctly."

"And what are the demographics?"

"Roughly seventy percent of the population is under the age of twenty-five. Male-to-female ratio is about forty-five to fifty-five."

"Good. So we have roughly thirty thousand to forty thousand males. Seventy percent of those are under the age of twenty-five. Do the math—you have several thousand potential fighters. So for the individual cells themselves, even if you kill most of the fighters, the leaders can simply recruit more. And even if the leader is killed, plenty more are out there to take their place. What size are most of the families?"

I was not sure, but most families were fairly large—six to ten children was the norm.

"And how would you feel if a foreigner came to your hometown and killed one of your family members?"

"It depended on what he was doing."

"Okay, let's just take the 'escalation of force' incidents—your unit had forty of them in a hundred and twenty days. That's at least forty people who had shots fired at them just for getting too close to your patrols. Let's see . . . there were thirty-seven civilian casualties from those incidents, including seventeen dead. What would you do if your family members, who were simply going about their daily business, were killed or wounded by a foreign force?"

I agreed that I would probably fight.

"Let's say, conservatively, that each of the civilians killed or wounded was related to three military-age males. That's more than one hundred people who may have decided to fight back. Those numbers alone make up for the networks you believe you eliminated. Now if we go to the air strike and the fallout from that . . ."

This was getting painful, but the point was made. And now I understood how Nargul got ugly—the Mir there, who had been peaceful before, joined the insurgency. I guess they did not really need anyone from Markhand after all.

"That's what I mean by COIN math. Your tactics are superb, but right now, the math is working against you. You inflicted a lot of flesh wounds. Plenty of individual tactical successes, but the dynamics of the conflict are getting away from you."

"Yes, more people were joining the insurgency than was the case when I started. Certainly not the kind of outcome I desired."

"Last question, how much do you know about Mirgul?"

"Only what the governor and police chief told me," was the unfortunate answer. I needed to get better visibility on exactly what was happening in Mirgul. All of my forces were in the main FOB. It was great for flexibility and to rotate missions among the companies, but I really had no idea what was going on outside the FOB—in Mirgul or any other village—other than what the governor and police chief told me.

"Maybe Naseem is not so dumb after all," Alex said.

My Key Lessons

Be wary of HUMINT (human intelligence) reports. Sometimes they are accurate, but people can use them to feed you all sorts of information and try to get you to be the bouncer in their personal disputes. Look before you leap . . . or strike.

Understand COIN math and the fact that reasonable operations that make perfect tactical sense to us can end up increasing support for insurgency. We need to adjust our procedures accordingly.

Get close to the people. Live near them—even among them—if you can. Get to know firsthand what is happening.

Understand the local situation—not just what is happening but why it is happening. People will often blame external actors in an effort to avoid close scrutiny of what is happening in the area. Although some agency is necessary to get an insurgency going, local support is often at the heart of it. Remove the local support, and the external agency has a much harder time gaining any traction.

"Okay, that's a reasonable start," said Alex. "What I suggest we do is reset the program to four days prior to the airstrike."

Mick concurred with the suggestion.

Getting to Know Mirgul

Mick and I talked together before I reentered the simulator. He had some additional pointers on tactics that he had forgotten to mention yesterday. He agreed that we needed to get a better picture of what was happening in Mirgul.

I said I intended to build an outpost near Mirgul so we could get to the village routinely and clear it of insurgents. Mick agreed and eagerly talked me though the finer points of building a combat outpost—machine-gun position emplacement, sectors of fire, primary and alternate command and control bunkers, trenches, and so on. "You have to dig; use the earth as your protection."

We pored over the map and selected a good spot for a company-size outpost just north of Mirgul. It was on relatively flat ground in a valley with the river to the west and mountains to the east. We also had great spots for two observation posts to overwatch the main camp—one that peered into the town and another that observed the rat line from Fargul to Sudgul, Nangul, and Balrok. Having the main outpost on low ground was not ideal, but it made logistical resupply much easier, as well as medical evacuation and access to Mirgul.

We then planned the mission to establish the outpost. We figured we would need about four days to build the initial positions. We used a standard program to determine the amount of supplies and equipment to order and coordinated for other "enablers," including UAV, fixed-wing support, a quick reaction force, and medical evacuation.

Making New Plans—Nargul Base

I reentered the simulator and got the wheels in motion to establish the new outpost. I had grown more cautious with Bar Pak and Al'a Dust and did not share the plans for the outpost with them immediately.

I began to question them about Bala Khan and their relationship. They said Bala Khan had stopped supporting the government over a year ago and was now a Takriri insurgent leader. He was jealous of Bar Pak and Al'a Dust and wanted all the power in the province to himself. The provincial council agreed with their assessment.

Two days before the operation I informed Bar Pak and Al'a Dust that I simply did not know enough about Mirgul and was worried about the insurgent activity coming from there. The outpost would be a "shaping" operation to get a greater understanding of insurgent activity in the town and stage forces to clear it and then get governance and development moving.

They suggested getting some civil servants and police trained to move into the town once it was cleared. I had not thought about that and welcomed the suggestion. Bar Pak and Al'a Dust immediately began selecting officials and police from the province for the mission.

An Encounter with Naseem

Meanwhile, I had asked Naseem for his opinion. "We should discuss this with the people and get their opinions," he said. "Then we can plan this together."

I informed him that the idea of talking with the people was both ridiculous and suicidal. They would attack us when we were most vulnerable. We needed the element of surprise for this to work.

"You know how to kill, commander," Naseem said. "But you do not know how to win."

"Excuse me?" I said, barely suppressing my anger.

"You have sight," he said, "but you do not see. You can hear, but you do not listen. You talk, but you do not communicate. If your map is wrong, you will be lost constantly."

I turned away in disgust. He must have broken out a box of fortune cookies and collected the messages.

I had no confidence in Naseem's staff to plan anything. We would just be wasting time by including them in the process.

"If you insist on this mission," he said, "I will need to get permission from my chain of command to put my soldiers in a new outpost."

I was growing impatient. Naseem said the Ministry of Defense needed to approve this, which could take weeks. This was a classic attempt to use the chain of command to avoid doing anything—the asking of permission had become a signal from a lower commander to his bosses that he was being asked to do something he did not want to do. In this way, the lower commander avoided conflict with his counterpart. Once his bosses said no, he would claim that his hands were tied.

Moving to Mirgul

I decided to launch the operation anyway and let the KNA catch up later, provided the bureaucrats allowed them to do so. I knew the answer to that already. It was no wonder they couldn't get anything done in this country. In this case, it was probably a good thing. Having us execute the initial mission alone would reduce the operational friction and the number of potential problems. Once the position was established and Mirgul was cleared, the KNA would probably agree to join us.

The operation to establish the outpost went without a hitch. We cut down a lot of trees to establish clear fields of fire and observation into Mirgul. We dug a well to access the water source—an aquifer ran underground, which was very helpful.

We were established, with all security, communications, and basic infrastructure set, within four days. Everything was going quite well with our side of the effort.

The people from Mirgul, however, were upset that we put an outpost so close to their village. They probably knew what was coming. We began routine patrols through the village, both day and night, scoping out compounds suspected of harboring insurgents.

People mainly went inside when our patrols came to the village. It was still summertime, so our vehicles kicked up a lot of dust in the town market as we drove through. Those who remained outside stared icily at us as they slapped away the settling dirt.

We began to see a few people make overtures toward us at night. They would give us some information on insurgent leaders in the village. Our picture of what was happening in the town was improving. As the people in Mirgul began to figure out that we were not going to be leaving anytime soon, they grew agitated. They began organizing protests outside the outpost, claiming stolen land. My company commander there showed them the approval from the government for the position, but that did not seem to matter. Direct-fire incidents on the outpost and observation posts increased.

When we began drilling pipes for latrines on the outpost—downstream from the well, of course—the outrage, and the contact, grew even more intense.

We began patrolling the village with greater frequency. We generally did not have direct-fire contact in the town itself but would receive it coming and going. Our operations, I assessed, had pushed most of the insurgents out of the town itself. They had to rely on conducting attacks in the countryside. This was good news—life support and resupply were more difficult in the countryside.

An Engagement in Balrok

Nonetheless, enemy contact remained high. One of my patrols was moving from the main outpost to the new base in Mirgul, passing through the tiny village of Balrok, when a large IED, packed in a drainage culvert, exploded underneath the third vehicle in the patrol. Thankfully, the crew escaped largely unhurt, even though the vehicle was destroyed.

My emotions ranged from relief that my soldiers were okay to intense anger that people would allow a large IED to be placed in the village itself. They had to know it was there—and they did nothing about it. The simply watched as our vehicles went right toward it.

I ordered a quick-reaction force to deploy from the Mirgul base to secure the site and evacuate any wounded. The platoon was scheduled to conduct a patrol to the Nargul base later that day so they were ready to move at short notice.

The QRF leader secured the site and reported that several large rocks from the detonation had damaged three or four buildings and a number of children had been harmed. He asked for some additional medical assistance, but we had none to spare and I was not going to bring the civilians on to one of our outposts. I directed that the ones with serious injuries be treated and the rest advised to go to the local clinic in Nargul.

The QRF leader used his combat trackers to follow footprints from the site to what appeared to be the hide-site of the triggerman. They followed footprints from there to a compound, searched it, and found three military-aged males and plenty of IED material.

I ordered him to secure the detainees and bring them to Nargul immediately for interrogation. The QRF leader responded that he wanted to spend additional time in the village. He reported that he was talking with the village's religious leader and a couple of elders, all of whom were upset by the incident. He thought we could use this engagement as an opportunity to gain popular support and give the insurgents a black eye.

I told him to recover the destroyed vehicle and get moving to Nargul. I wanted the detainees, and the patrol needed to secure supplies and mail for the soldiers in Mirgul. I wanted them to have time to get back to Mirgul by nightfall. The thought of using the incident to turn the people in this minor village in our favor was a naïve waste of time that could put the soldiers in further danger in a nighttime movement back to Mirgul.

He pleaded for more time to talk with the people and treat the wounded children. I grew impatient and ordered him to move out immediately or I would relieve him.

Clearing Mirgul

Even though violence in the area remained high, the shift of enemy contact away from the Mirgul population center indicated that our efforts were working. The insurgents were losing the support of the people. My staff developed a PowerPoint presentation showing the change, which the brigade used in their briefings as evidence of progress.

Our increased situational awareness of the town improved our ability to plan a very precise mission to remove the key insurgent leaders. Once they were cleared from the town, we could get governance and development working.

I decided the clearing operation could not wait any longer. I wanted to capitalize on the momentum we were building. The KNA still had not gotten permission to occupy the position. We would have to use the police to put a "Khanastan face" on the operation.

We divided the town into five objectives and hit them all at once at night. It was a textbook cordon-and-search operation. Al'a Dust's police set up the outer cordon with some of my forces. We provided the majority of the assault forces to clear the objectives—the mission was too important to get the unevenly trained police heavily involved.

Mick provided some mentoring on the operation during a short break. We conducted what he called a "deep clear"—we searched every house and business in the town over the course of three days. No one entered the town; no one left it. We had a complete lockdown.

A number of firefights erupted during the house-to-house searches. We found several caches of weapons and ammunition and two IED factories. We killed about fifty insurgents overall and captured several hundred. We followed the standard protocol of blindfolding them or putting bags over their heads and hauling them away in trucks for interrogation. I wanted to detain and question as many as possible, so we cast a wide net.

To avoid the COIN math problem, I ensured each of them was treated well during confinement and released once we had finished questioning and had no reason to hold them any longer.

We learned that Bala Khan had left the village two nights earlier. We clearly had a leak.

The town was quiet for about ten days or so, then fighting erupted again. We spent the next several weeks mired in the "clear" phase. IEDs and complex attacks began to increase. We were taking the fight to the enemy in his own backyard, so violence was increasing.

To get other efforts moving concurrently, we deployed the "government in a box" concept—the civil servants and police that had just emerged from training were delivered as a package to the town. Al'a Dust and I placed police checkpoints throughout the town and around the municipal governor's office. I had hoped once we got some law and order, proper governance, and money into the area, we would start making progress. I was determined to move into the "hold" phase as quickly as possible.

The new municipal governor held a council with the elders. I noticed that the same people who had stepped up to provide information to us were among the new local leaders. That was comforting. The governor seemed very dedicated to his job. Bar Pak was impressed with him. We continued precise kill-capture operations against various insurgent leaders who emerged in the area. I was careful to avoid collateral damage in order to prevent the COIN math problem. We were decimating the networks.

Violence began to subside against us, but it began in earnest against the police. Insurgents were hitting them day and night. Fourteen were killed in three days. The police must have been doing their jobs right to get that kind of reaction.

The KNA, meanwhile, refused to grant permission for some of their forces to occupy the Mirgul outpost. Naseem apologized for this. I thought maybe it was for the best—they risked being worse than useless in this environment.

I decided to reinforce the police and put additional protection around the municipal governor. After a couple of elders were threatened by the insurgents, no one came to the governor's meetings any longer. I was getting frustrated.

We recleared the town—I think this was the third time. We did not get any contact this time, nor did we find weapons caches and IED factories. We did have six soldiers killed in four separate "house IEDs"—the insurgents had wired the entrances with explosives. When we kicked in the doors, the bombs detonated.

That pissed me off even more. I began to think Mirgul was a lost cause. No matter what we did, the people resisted. The municipal governor left; the police abandoned their posts. I withdrew the remaining joint checkpoints—I did not want to leave my men in the town alone.

The next two weeks were quiet. Reporting had dried up.

Then all hell broke loose.

The Fight at Mirgul COP

"Contact!" screamed the radio operator from the northern observation post. The contact report from the southern OP came moments later. The main combat outpost was also receiving direct fire and mortars—

pinning us down so we could not send immediate reinforcements to the OPs. My FOB was also under a direct-fire and rocket attack from the southeast.

About one hundred insurgents converged on each outpost. Direct fire started from one direction on each OP. Suicide bombers threw themselves at the gates. We shifted forces to counter the attacks and began hammering away at their positions.

These attacks, however, were diversions, designed to fix our attention in one direction along the most obvious avenue of approach. More suicide bombers flung themselves on the opposite side of the OPs to create a breach through which insurgents poured in. My soldiers fought for their lives at close quarters, calling in airstrikes and strafing runs right in front of their positions. They fought heroically.

I committed the quick-reaction force from Nargul, which made good time until getting hung up on IED belts five kilometers north of the outpost near Balrok. As they finally made their way through and onto the outpost—with three dead and five critically injured—the firefight subsided and the remaining insurgents withdrew.

The two OPs were nearly overrun. My men had stood their ground but paid a heavy price. In addition to the QRF casualties, we had seven killed and six wounded at the northern OP, and eight killed and four wounded at the southern OP. Two were killed and eight wounded in the Mirgul outpost. The company was combat ineffective. Now I was really upset at Naseem and the KNA. They had abandoned us in a difficult mission. Their presence might have kept some of my soldiers alive.

The scenario paused, and I emerged from the simulator shaking my head in frustration. Once again, I thought, I had done everything right. I selected the best location available for the outpost and set up two observation posts for added protection. We had done a textbook clearing operation, killed a number of insurgents, found weapons caches and IED factories. We deployed government officials and police. I took extra care to ensure detainees were well treated.

Mick seemed upset as well. Like me, he could not understand what went wrong. He persisted in the belief that the system was flawed and creating perverse outcomes.

Initial Debrief

Alex came down to where Mick and I were seated. "Okay, another tough mission. What do you think happened, and why did it happen?"

I explained my decision-making process. I had wanted to get better visibility on Mirgul prior to a clearance operation. I had established a combat outpost and two observation posts to standard, conducted clearing operations, established governance and police presence, and treated detainees well. Then things erupted.

Alex began a series of questions. "What considerations did you examine in selecting the outpost location?"

"I looked for a place with the easiest access to the road, in proximity to the village, and that was relatively flat. We cleared fields of fire and observation and established two OPs for added security. We dug a well, hardened our positions, and so on. It was the best place in the area."

"What did Naseem think of the operation?"

"He seemed to support it, but he could not get permission from the KNA to participate. He made the foolish suggestion of talking with the people first. I think that idea simply would have created a bigger attack earlier in the mission—we would have been revealing our plans to the enemy."

"How did the people of Mirgul feel about it?"

"They were clearly upset."

Alex persisted. "Why?"

Mick was losing patience. "Because the Jammers didn't want them so close! Jeez, Alex, why do you keep giving him the third degree? The simulation is obviously flawed. He did everything right."

I thought Mick had as good an explanation as any. I didn't know any other reason for them to be so upset.

Alex tried a difference approach. "Why do you think violence in the town decreased at one point?"

"That was a clear sign," I said, "that the people were turning against the insurgents. The enemy no longer had enough support from the village after we did the initial clearing operations and the governor got the council together. The fighters had to leave and try to fight their way back in from the outside."

"What happened next?"

"We did the clearing operation to take out the remaining leadership. Killed plenty of insurgents, took some detainees, found weapons and IED caches. We met with some elders and brought in a governor and police."

"Let's take a look at some of those points," said Alex. "You conducted a textbook cordon and search. What were you trying to accomplish?"

"We wanted to clear the town of insurgent presence," I answered. "Once we got rid of the insurgents, we could then bring in governance, followed by development."

"How well did that work out?"

"The mission went very well, but we wound up having to repeat it two more times. The insurgents seemed to have regenerated inside the village. I still cannot account for that. Each time we thought we had successfully cleared the town, the insurgents came back stronger."

"To what do you attribute that strength?" Alex asked.

"I'm sure it had something to do with COIN math, but I don't understand what was happening behind the scenes to build that regenerative capacity."

"Right," said Alex. "The notion of 'clear' is a bit of a misnomer in a local insurgency."

That began to make sense. If the insurgents were nonlocal, "clearing" the area of that external presence was plausible. If, however, they were locals, then most of them would go to ground, hide their weapons, and wait until we were cleared out of the area to resume activity.

"That's a tough problem. We'll try to get more insight from the readout." Alex continued, "Let's explore the next issue. You met with some elders—do you know their story and why they met with you?"

"They said they were the leaders of the town. Some looked pretty young. I am not quite sure, looking back on it, why they would only meet at night."

"Good question! After all, if the insurgency is local and these people are the town leaders, they should be able to meet with you more openly," observed Alex.

Yes, there was certainly something more to the story than met the eye.

Alex pressed on. "A local governor was brought in to the town. He had some civil service training, which is good news. How effective was he?"

"We initially thought he would work out well," I recounted. "He met with the elders that had talked with us. But he never seemed to get any traction with the people. Once the intimidation campaign began, his days were numbered. The new police fared little better, and soon left altogether."

"Why did he have problems getting traction?"

I didn't have answer for that. We did everything by the book. We cleared the area, established a degree of security. We thickened the "hold" forces by bringing in police and brought governance. Development would follow later.

"You did bring in govern*ment,*" explained Alex. "Whether that was gover*nance* is a different question."

"Are we splitting hairs again, Alex?" asked Mick. "Our job is security. We kill or capture insurgents, clear the area, thicken security; then it is the government's job to bring governance and development. We can help to a degree, but it is really not our lane."

"Maybe not, strictly speaking, but the distinction is important. Gover*ment* is about officials and positions. Gover*nance* is about decision making, problem solving, and consensus building. It is about responsibility and accountability to the people. Official government plays a role in that, but not the only role. How we help facilitate credible government to provide effective governance is important."

I really had not done much to support the governor. My troops did their jobs, and I expected him to do his. I did not want to interfere in what he was doing, but we should have figured out ways to work together.

"Okay, one thing you said struck me," Alex said as he took his characteristic deep breath to emphasize a point. "You talk about security, governance, and development as sequential activities. The old manual certainly implies that. Is it possible that lack of governance or economic opportunity can create security problems? Should we think of these as sequential or concurrent activities?"

I had not thought of it like that before. We discussed various examples of how the lack of a local governance mechanism eroded a community's ability to solve problems short of violence, and how the exclusion of various groups from decision making could create an incentive for the groups to resort to violence.

"Not all violence is due to ideology," Alex observed. "Particularly in a local insurgency, much of the violence has more practical, local issues and grievances as the underlying causes."

Mick interjected, "You're demanding a lot of our counterinsurgents, Alex. Probably more than they can reasonably handle. There is much to be said for focusing on what we do well—security—and not getting distracted by these other issues. At some point, if you try to do too much, you wind up doing a lot of everything poorly."

"That's a reasonable point. However, if we do not understand the nature of the conflict and why people are supporting insurgency and violence, we will continue to apply the wrong solutions," Alex replied. "Not every problem is a nail that requires a hammer.

"One final point," he continued. "What did you make of the IED incident in Balrok when your QRF leader was trying to talk with the locals?"

I had nearly forgotten about that incident—it seemed so minor at the time. The QRF leader thought he could turn the incident into a black eye for the insurgents. We needed to get the damaged vehicle and detainees out of there, and the patrol had another mission to accomplish before nightfall.

"Any idea who he was talking with?" Alex inquired.

"A religious leader and a couple of elders, I think. We treated some of the more seriously wounded and then moved on. A lot of good those efforts did—we just got more IEDs."

Alex was clearly unsurprised by the outcome. He had no "special knowledge" of the situation—nothing more than Mick and I knew—but he had a sixth sense of how things connected that I was growing to respect.

Feedback Session

The technical experts had sorted through all the data and feedback loops. At Mick's insistence, they checked again for glitches in the system and found none. The game was operating as designed.

The people of Mirgul rose in opposition to the outpost because they believed it threatened their lives. The outpost was built on some of the scarce arable land near the town. The appropriation of their land for the outpost cut severely into the food supply. As fruit trees were cut down to improve fields of fire, food supply and economic livelihood were affected further. The reduction in crops increased the cost of food. With the vast unemployment in the area, it meant that people were less able to afford to feed their families.

The outpost was also placed along the main aquifer that supplies fresh water to the town. The well at the outpost threatened the water supply in the village. When latrine pipes were constructed, the threatened water supply risked contamination.

Naseem was clearly concerned about the operation and the potential blowback from the population. That is why he suggested you speak with them first. He registered his concerns with the KNA brigade commander, who said that he would ensure the Ministry of Defense disapproved of KNA participation in the operation.

Those representing themselves as Mirgul "elders" were really opportunists looking to make money and gain influence by befriending you. The townspeople believed that these self-appointed elders were selling the people out for personal gain and grew very angry. That is why these so-called "elders" would meet only at night.

Meanwhile, the real elders got together and decided that they should try to avoid fighting in the village. A general principle among the people is that fighting in a village in the presence of families and children is indecent. They did not want to do more harm to the village. As a result, violence moved away from the town and into the countryside.

The incident in Balrok was an exception. The people were really upset that the insurgents put an IED in the town and harmed a number of children. Tactically, the choke point was a good location for the IED, but it almost cost the insurgents dearly.

Your patrol leader was talking with some influential elders—he did not quite know how influential they were, but sensed that he was making some progress. He explained that he was horrified at the disregard for the people—he was less concerned about the damaged vehicle and more concerned about the children. When he was ordered back to Nargul abruptly, people thought all the talk from the Americans was empty—that all they cared about were themselves. There were no more IEDs in Balrok, but the people did not stop IED activity outside the town.

Back in Mirgul, once the governor and police arrived, the people believed that the government was trying to use these self-appointed leaders to overthrow the tribal leaders.

The real elders, led by Bala Khan, began the intimidation campaign to scare off these "pretenders" and get rid of the police. They weathered the "clearing operations" by hiding their weapons—fighting back in the village did them more harm than good. They also preserved their force by reducing the lower-level attacks against the outpost and OPs.

They adapted their strategy to remove the easier threats first—the governor and police—so they could concentrate on the larger threat to the town. Then they massed forces against your positions; many figured they were at risk of starving anyway and preferred to fight while they had the chance. Bala Khan had no problem recruiting fighters. The entire town rose up.

I was stunned. The logic of it all made such perfect sense. It was so simple. We had done everything "right" but everything we did was counterproductive because we did not understand the real impact of what we were doing. Decisions that were tactically sound wound up inflaming the insurgency. I was beginning to internalize that lesson.

"There are two laws that operate with iron consistency in most counterinsurgencies: the law of gravity, and the law of unintended consequences," observed Alex, as he came back down to the debriefing area.

Mick was clearly troubled, bothered by something. He looked darkly at the report, perhaps recalling some past experiences.

Alex began, "What are your thoughts on this?"

"Everything we did backfired on us. The selection of the combat outpost and observation posts, cutting down fruit trees to clear fields of fire, the well and latrines, the lost opportunity in Balrok, the cordon-and-search operations . . . We made good decisions from a purely tactical sense, but everything we did angered the population. We essentially took a volatile situation and threw gasoline on it."

"Let's focus on a few key areas. You clearly get the fact that the best decisions from a purely military standpoint can wind up doing more harm than good. So how do we get close to Mirgul—which is the right move, I think—without generating such backlash?"

"We need to know more about the area—the geography, the people and their social and political issues, how they make their livelihood—and to think through the ramifications of emplacing new positions."

"Good. Perhaps Naseem was right about talking to the people. Your presence is going to affect them in various ways—not all of which you can anticipate. You cannot eliminate all of the adverse consequences."

"Exactly, but we can learn enough to avoid making disastrous decisions like I made earlier. We can also think through how we compensate people for the loss of land and other issues."

"Now you're starting to sound like a social worker instead of a soldier," chided Mick. "The security benefits and promise of future development should be compensation enough for them."

"Let's explore that," said Alex.

I think this was the first time I considered disagreeing with Mick. We discussed the fact that this is a conflict-ridden society. Survival is the people's top consideration. When people perceive a choice between survival in the near term and vague promises of benefits in the long term, they are likely to choose survival first—they might not be around to enjoy the future. From their viewpoint, anything perceived to threaten survival needs to be addressed, even if it comes at the cost of longer-term benefits. Part of our job, then, was to help assure immediate survival and address basic livelihood concerns while also keeping future opportunities open.

"I think you are right. We need to avoid creating false choices, or putting people in a position in which their best choice is armed opposition to our efforts."

I needed to do a better job learning before leaping into something.

My Key Lessons

Know yourself, know the enemy, know the environment. Sometimes decisions that are optimal from a military standpoint can undermine our efforts. We need to analyze our decisions from the perspective of the population, not just our own considerations. Sometimes the best military tactics have short-term gains but create long-term problems.

Security, governance, economic support, and public information are interconnected. You have to integrate them, not treat them as separate and distinct efforts. Sometimes the best way to improve security is through effective governance and economic opportunity.

Counterinsurgency requires a purposeful blend of violent and nonviolent efforts. The art of counterinsurgency, in part, is getting the blend right enough to accomplish your objectives.

Winning Hearts and Minds—Comprehending Comprehensive COIN

L ike most officers, I generally did not read manuals, theory and history of warfare, or academic works from other disciplines. I always thought that was "geek stuff" and a distraction from training my soldiers. This lack of intellectual curiosity was starting to haunt me.

Over the weekend break, I pulled out the old counterinsurgency manual and actually read it . . . twice. I was familiar with the boilerplate mantra of security, governance, development, and information, but never considered in much detail how to apply the nonsecurity and nonlethal factors or integrate them.

I needed to take a more "comprehensive" approach to what we were doing. While security was job one, without the other elements, our efforts would amount to little more than simple attrition of militants. And since the number of military-age youth was so large, the militants would just regenerate. The insurgency had an elastic quality—the more violence and problems we brought, the more fighters would materialize to confront them.

We would be like rats in a wheel—producing a lot of frenetic activity, but no real progress. I finally began to understand what old General Petraeus meant when he said that you cannot kill your way out of an insurgency.

I decided to place a much heavier focus on the other elements of counterinsurgency. I organized a portion of my staff to deal with those issues. I wanted to make governance work and get some development projects going. I also needed to communicate better with the people. We needed to win hearts and minds.

A New Plan at Nargul Base

We agreed to rewind the game to the decision to emplace the outpost near Mirgul. I knew where *not* to put the outpost this time, but was uncertain of a better location. I decided to consult with Naseem, Bar Pak and Al'a Dust.

"This flat ground here would be a good option." Bar Pak was pointing on the map where we had placed the outpost last time. Al'a Dust shook his head, "The farmland in the area is scarce, and that is a key plot. The aquifers also run underneath. We need to find a different place." Naseem agreed.

This was interesting. Bar Pak was not from the local area, so perhaps he was just ignorant of those issues. But if he did not understand such fundamental aspects of the area, what else did he not know? If he did know, then his advice had some darker purpose. I wanted to give him the benefit of the doubt, so I chalked it up to ignorance. I needed to help him get out to the people in the province more often.

Bar Pak apologized quickly for making such a bad suggestion. Al'a Dust said he had fought in these areas for many years. "You want a place that you can defend easily—or at least that the enemy will have a very difficult time attacking—and that gives you good access to the town and road and that will not threaten the population. Here are some places to consider."

Al'a Dust pointed his thick finger to a couple areas. "I have fought in each one of these. We had positions there during the wars with Markhand. This one here is near the road and village, but is at the bottom of the valley. The terrain is steep and there is little concealment. With observation posts here and here, you can keep the enemy off the high ground. You will need to send out security patrols constantly to prevent small groups from coming too close."

Naseem explained that his forces had used similar tactics during the wars.

The position made me nervous when Al'a Dust first mentioned it, but I began to visualize how it could work. We would need to patrol actively from the main outpost and the two observation posts to keep the enemy off balance. Staging a mass attack against the positions would be really difficult as long as we stayed active and employed the right force-protection measures.

Naseem and I reconnoitered the area with Al'a Dust and found the position as he described it—a tight position, but difficult to attack, especially with the observation posts and active patrolling. It was also far less disruptive to the population than our previous position while still giving us good access to Mirgul, the road, and adjacent villages.

We looked over some other positions as well. I trusted Al'a Dust to a point but did not want to show our hand too early. He might tell someone in confidence, who would then tell someone else in confidence, and so on until the word got to the wrong ears.

At Naseem's recommendation, I also prepared compensation for the loss of land—someone would invariably claim it. We felt a little compensation would generate good will and take the edge off our sudden occupation of the place. A little money was far less costly than the life or limb of one of my men.

"Are you seriously considering such a terrible position?" Mick was concerned about the decision and paused the game temporarily to discuss it. "I like the original location much better. You have a duty to your soldiers to select the most defensible position. Being concerned about the population is one thing, but putting your soldiers in a difficult-to-defend position is irresponsible. You have every right to seize the land you want—the government needs to figure out how to make it work for the people."

Mick was registering some of the same concerns my company commander was about the position. The commander had a good plan for base defense and force protection, but he was very nervous about it. Still, I knew what had happened the last time I occupied the best tactical position—it had cost us and the mission dearly. I had little faith Bar Pak had the resources or credibility to do anything to make that position work.

Not wanting to upset Mick, I said that I was just going to try this position. The good thing about a simulation is that no one really gets hurt and we can experiment with different solutions. Mick shook his head in resignation and went back down to his seat.

The old counterinsurgency manual also emphasized the importance of government legitimacy. I needed to determine ways to make Bar Pak

more legitimate in the eyes of the people. He clearly had limited understanding of the people in the Mirgul area. I wanted to help him get
access to them. I also wanted to show the people that we supported him
and that he could provide benefits to them. I needed to get him in the
game.

The manual also mentioned development. This is something I had
always delegated to my civil affairs team—never paying much attention
to it myself. Now I wanted to show the people in Mirgul and surrounding
villages that we could bring prosperity to them. I directed my civil
affairs team to draw up plans for projects in the area.

The civil affairs team developed proposals for several projects: a
250-kilowatt micro-hydro plant that would use river power to provide
electricity to the village, an access road that connected the main road to
the base and to the village to make our travel easier, a couple of schools,
a pipe scheme to bring water from a spring to two nearby villages, and a
water well. We would also widen the main road to improve the foundation for economic growth. That was as much as my immediate budget
would support.

To promote Bar Pak's legitimacy, I asked him if he knew any contractors that could build these facilities. He knew some excellent businesses from his home city of Ashrabad that could do the work. I also got
some engineer support to dig the well—I wanted us to get credit for that
and let Bar Pak have the credit for the rest.

Hearts and Minds in Mirgul

Naseem was far more helpful now. He agreed to provide a company to
the Mirgul outpost and supporting observation posts. He urged me to get
the local people involved in the projects and cautioned against allowing
Bar Pak to influence the developmental decisions because of concerns
about corruption, but I believed that improving his legitimacy was worth
the risk.

Once we had the force-protection resources lined up and development contracts sorted out, we conducted the tactical mission to occupy
the outpost and two observations posts. The mission itself went smoothly,
and within four days we had established the positions with barrier material, overhead cover, reinforced bunkers, and interlocking fields of fire.

We had some initial firefights from the village, but the fighting in the immediate area stopped once the insurgents knew they could not dislodge our positions. The fighting then moved away from the village areas. I took this as a sign that the people had an open mind about our new positions and forced the insurgents out of the village.

The people of Mirgul remained relatively quiet as we occupied the area. We found plenty of shell casings and some old personal equipment from the wars of the last two decades as we dug the positions. The places had clearly been used before, as Al'a Dust had said.

Because the outpost was on the south side of the village, we had to drive through the Mirgul bazaar to get to the base.

On one of the trips, I decided to take Bar Pak so he could talk to the people. We stopped in the middle of the bazaar, established security, and pushed the crowd to the outer perimeter.

Bar Pak strode proudly through the bazaar, flanked by Al'a Dust's policemen and my security detail. He explained to the people that he was going to widen the main road and provide electricity and two schools to the area, with the promise of more to come. He was also going to have a pipe scheme built to bring water to nearby villages. I had given him a lot of humanitarian assistance—mainly rice and wheat—which he handed out to various people. I explained that we fully supported the governor and police and would work through them for the people of Mirgul. I also said we would be digging wells in villages so people would not have to walk so far to get water.

The people of Mirgul remained silent through the speeches. One elderly man asked who would build all of these things. Bar Pak replied that he would bring in the best businessmen and skilled labor from Ashrabad, and that they would employ some of the people in Mirgul.

So far, so good. We had a few sporadic attacks on the outpost and observation posts, but our patrolling really kept the insurgents off balance. The positions we occupied were far more defensible than they had initially looked, provided we stayed active. The insurgents had a really hard time trying to get rockets to land on the base—most simply flew overhead.

I was worried about mortars, so I put a counter-mortar radar at one of the observation posts. The radar would acquire the round at two points—when it went up and when it came down. Based on the data from the two intersections, the radar could determine the insurgent firing point, which enabled us to fire back at them accurately.

Various individuals from Mirgul began to visit the outpost looking for jobs. I kept bringing Bar Pak back to the town about once a week or so. He began building some relationships with people, who formed a town council. Bar Pak selected a council leader from the group.

Construction began on the development projects. The businessmen Bar Pak hired brought a lot of skilled and some unskilled labor with them. The town council selected some men to supplement the work.

After a few months, the projects were under way and some nearing completion. The canal for the micro-hydro plant was built and the turbine was on hand. A school for Mirgul was being constructed near our base; this would add protection for the facility. Another school was placed between the villages of Sudgul and Fargul, which were further up one of the valleys; we figured the one school could service both villages. A pipe scheme would also service the villages in that valley. We dug a well in Mirgul and in the nearby village of Hamrok.

The road projects were having some problems. For some reason, people began protesting the road widening. The town council said they were just malcontents who did not know what was good for them. We also ran into a lot of resistance on the access road from the outpost to Mirgul. Threatening letters were left on the equipment, and workers were getting beaten up. When one of the contractors was murdered on his way to work, the project stopped.

We continued crediting Bar Pak for all of the work being done in the area. The town council was pleased. Every once in a while, a villager would complain that the projects were being built poorly. Bar Pak and the council said these were just disgruntled people who griped about everything.

Naseem thought we should create a mechanism to hear their complaints. He also cautioned that we should help ensure the council was politically inclusive—not made up of just one social group or of hand-picked men. I agreed and asked Bar Pak to look at the makeup of the council and address complaints.

Despite all of this work, the area remained hostile—although not as bad as in the previous scenarios. The Mirgul bazaar was generally empty when we showed up, and most businesses closed their doors. IEDs and ambushes continued on the road between our main base to the north and the Mirgul outpost. Nonetheless, the governor was now actively engaged with the people and projects were ongoing. I continued to explain to people that we and the government were there to help them and that more benefits would come if they told us where the insurgents were hiding.

Ribbon Cutting in Nangul and Other Finished Projects

The first project to be completed was the pipe scheme. The pipes ran from a mountain spring to the villages of Nangul and Sudgul. Now the people would not have to travel to the spring to get their water, they could simply use the tap in the village center. We decided to have a ribbon-cutting ceremony in Nangul, which was closer to the base and easier to secure.

Bar Pak made a speech about how the government was supporting the people and how proud he was to open the pipe scheme. I was there as well with my company commander, Police Chief Al'a Dust, Naseem, and the contractor.

During the governor's speech, a couple of elders began yelling at Bar Pak. Other elders yelled back at them, and a fight broke out. I had no idea what was happening but alerted my men of the security threat. Al'a Dust punched one of the elders, knocking him down. The police arrested the hecklers and led them out of the area in flexcuffs. The governor finished his speech, the contractor opened the spigot, letting out a steady stream of water. We cut the ribbon and took pictures to put in our local newsletter.

On the way back to the outpost, I asked Bar Pak and Al'a Dust what happened. They said some people from Fargul were upset with the pipe scheme because it did not come to their village. But Fargul was closest to the spring, so they really did not need the pipes. Some people, Bar Pak explained, will never be satisfied.

I hoped the people of Fargul would be satisfied with the school that was being built in the area, between their village and Sudgul.

We finished the wells in Mirgul and Hamrok a couple weeks later. We had put the Mirgul well on the north side of town, as the council suggested. We also had the contractor build some irrigation ditches and water-flow control points at selected places so the people could divert water to the fields as necessary. Improving the harvest would be good for the local economy, and the town council was very excited about the project. The Hamrok well was built in the middle of the village. The women of the town used to walk two kilometers to the spring to fetch water. Now they could stay in the village and spend time doing other things.

I noticed that the women played little to no apparent role in village decision making. This was bad from a practical standpoint—fifty-five percent of the people were women—and I was concerned about the human rights side of it as well. I encouraged Bar Pak to bring women onto the town and provincial councils. He said that he would discuss the matter with the people. I insisted that he make this a priority—we were getting very clear guidance from the embassy about women's inclusion.

The road-widening project continued to face problems. We patrolled the road constantly and sent out flyers about the prosperity a widened road would bring to the people, but the IEDs and ambushes kept up at a steady rate. I was growing concerned. At the same time, I got a report that the pipe scheme was no longer working. I suspected that the people of Fargul had damaged it.

The school between Fargul and Sudgul was finally finished, as was the school near the Mirgul outpost. The opening ceremony for the Mirgul school was attended by the town council. It went off well, but I had been hoping for greater attendance. Just a handful of students, mainly poor children who lived near the base, used the school in the following weeks. That was disappointing, but at least it was a start.

My company commander at the Mirgul base was receiving a lot of complaints about the quality of the work and reports that Bar Pak was stealing money. Naseem and his officers were getting similar reports. I dismissed most of that as sour grapes. Nassem kept pressing for a method for people to register complaints. I said that Bar Pak and the town council were supposed to deal with that, but Naseem believed this was inadequate.

The school between Fargul and Sudgul was vandalized a couple days after it was completed. Once again, I suspected the people of Fargul were behind it. We offered to pay to have it repaired, but the contractor said he refused to work there anymore because of security problems.

The Mirgul micro-hydro plant was finally finished. I was very excited about this. Electricity was one of those very visible signs of progress. It also provided an important foundation for future economic development.

The opening ceremony was fairly well attended. Even though Mirgul was generally unfriendly, this was a potentially transformative project. Even some of the malcontents seemed interested. The stakes were pretty high, so I was relieved when lights in the bazaar turned on—and stayed on.

A few days later, my company commander received a report that the Hamrok well was damaged. The insurgents were obviously unhappy about the work we did . . . and I was unhappy that the work we had done for the village, and for the women, was now in ruins.

Meanwhile, the attacks on the road-widening project continued. The contractor refused to work any longer. The local workforce had quit several weeks ago, and now the nonlocals were being targeted. Attacks on the school between Sudgul and Fargul continued. We could not get anyone to repair the pipe scheme.

I was growing frustrated. I was doing everything the counterinsurgency manual said to do. I was promoting the governor at every opportunity, giving him credit for all of the work. I took him to visit many villages, standing by his side at every speech, ground-breaking, and ribbon-cutting ceremony. Sure, he was corrupt, but I had to work with him and improve the legitimacy of the government.

I had better success getting women on the town council by linking their participation to development money. Naseem once again urged caution on this issue. He said he supported a greater role for women, but said the women's participation on the council should be a local decision, not one imposed from outside. This seemed to me another example of him trying to have it both ways—avoid a fight with me while making a recommendation for local autonomy on the issue which he knew would result in rejecting women's participation.

Outcomes in Mirgul

I had poured money into the area to bring prosperity. We had attempted a number of projects, but they just got attacked each time. Didn't the people appreciate what we were giving them?

Naseem continued to advocate for the people in Mirgul to have a greater role, but Bar Pak and I both believed that they lacked the skills necessary to build quality projects.

I distributed flyers to the people, explaining the great benefits that we and the government were bringing to the area. We had coordinated talking points so the right messages got out.

I did not want to do another major kinetic operation in Mirgul, but the situation was beginning to get out of hand. Bala Khan's support had been growing despite our efforts. He said we brought only misery and destruction. The government was corrupt and stealing money from the people. The projects were a sham. Our discussions about bringing women onto the council were described as cultural imperialism.

The sporadic attacks on the Mirgul outpost and the two observation posts were not very effective but of enough concern that we focused several air-assault missions into the mountains to disrupt reported insurgent staging areas and command-and-control locations. These missions normally generated a brief firefight, and then the fighters melted away. The missions also kept our attention away from the population. Our growing distance from the people, the constant disruption of the projects, the lack of popular support, and the increasing restrictions on our own freedom of movement were undermining our efforts.

The environment worsened when the Mirgul micro-hydro plant's canal eroded and mostly washed away after a rainstorm. The lights went out in the town.

An earthquake shook the area a week later. The Mirgul school collapsed. Twenty of the thirty children in the school died, most of them girls. When the earthquake began, a number of the boys had jumped out of the windows to get out of the building. The girls had huddled together in the center of the room. The falling roof crushed them. It was heartbreaking.

The people of Mirgul blamed Bar Pak and me for the deaths. They said they had warned us about the poor workmanship, and now twenty children were dead because we allowed shoddy construction of the school. People protested at the Mirgul outpost and the battalion base. Our credibility was waning rapidly.

"Stop the simulation! This is ridiculous." Mick Lundy was beside himself. "When are you going to teach these ungrateful people a lesson? Mirgul and these other villages are insurgent breeding factories—they are Tak-supporting Jammers! And you are throwing money at them. And for what? They take your money and then attack your projects and your soldiers. Why are you listening to this 'hearts and minds' crap? You need to clear Mirgul ASAP."

Alex was making his way down to us as Mick finished "counseling" me. "He tried all this sissy stuff about being nice and 'winning hearts and minds' and it did not work," Mick declared.

"No glitches in the system this time, Mick?" Alex chuckled.

I thought Mick was a bit over the top, but he did have a point. Although we did not have a major calamity involving lots of casualties this time, the situation was getting worse over time rather than better. I had followed the old counterinsurgency manual, and it did not seem to be doing a lot of good. I was not confident that a cordon and search to clear Mirgul would be beneficial in the long run, but I was running out of options and did not know what else to do.

Initial Debrief

"Okay," Alex clapped, "I think this is a good point to pause and determine a way forward. Describe what happened and why you think it happened."

I recounted how I had read the old counterinsurgency manual and tried to take a very different approach this time. I wanted to focus on governance, development, and information operations rather than just kinetic operations in villages. But the insurgency was gaining strength, although not as rapidly as it had in the other scenarios.

The selection of the outpost went better than expected. The people of Mirgul were not thrilled to have us there, but we did not suffer a major attack like last time. The positions were more defensible than I expected and did not cause major disruptions to the population.

The population had seemed to turn against the insurgents. Violence was initially concentrated in Mirgul, but once we established our positions, the violence moved into the countryside. I took this as a sign the population was supportive of, or at least not actively opposing, our presence.

With that part going well, I turned my focus to building government legitimacy and economic development. Things started going downhill after that.

Alex took a deep breath. "Well, let's start with building government legitimacy—how did you intend to do that?"

I explained how the manual discussed the importance of government legitimacy. I needed to get Bar Pak out to see the people and show them that we fully supported him. I coordinated all of the development projects with him; he even selected the contractors to ensure we got quality engineers and businessmen. He worked with the Mirgul town council. I wanted people to know that he was in charge and that we were there to support him in every way.

"How did the people feel about Bar Pak?" asked Alex.

"I don't know for sure. He never attracted much of a crowd when we took him from place to place or at major events. There were allegations of corruption, but I never paid much attention to them. I'm sure he *was* corrupt—just like the rest of the government officials. It's just the nature of this place."

"Remember last time we discussed the difference between govern-*ment* and gover*nance?*"

I did, but it still seemed to me like a distinction without a difference. The government is supposed to govern—to provide governance.

Alex pressed the point. "So how do you define governance?"

"The act of governing by the government!" Mick sneered as he said this, but Alex did not pay much attention.

"Governance is about decision making, problem solving, dispute resolution, and ensuring the needs of the governed are met," I answered.

"Does that mean all of the governed or just a few of them in this society?" continued Alex.

"It should be all of them, including the women," I said. But given that there was an insurgency in the area, there were certainly some who believed the government was not working for them.

Alex shifted the subject slightly, "How do communities here traditionally make decisions?"

"They form councils that operate on consensus. They can often discuss things for years until they gain consensus for a decision."

"It's no wonder why they never get anything done." Mick was clearly irritated.

"How are these councils constituted?" Alex asked.

"They are traditionally elected by the people within each social or tribal group. A traditional council has proportional representation among all groups, so every group's needs are represented and benefits are equitably distributed."

"Great!" Alex began bringing a few governance strands together, "So how well are Bar Pak and the Mirgul council doing against that standard?"

I did not really know. Mirgul had a council that worked together with Bar Pak. I never really determined whether all of the different groups were represented. They were almost all from the Mir tribe. I knew there were no women on the council, despite our advocacy, until we forced the issue.

"Do the Mir have any social subdivisions?" Alex inquired, "Are there any religious differences?"

"Come on, Alex, he's a soldier, not an anthropologist!" cried Mick.

I did have a "human terrain team" with the battalion—a bunch of egghead anthropologists. They gave me a rundown of the various subtribes and clans, which I thought was mildly interesting. But when I asked them what it meant and how to apply the information, they just shrugged and said they did not know—that was up to me to decide. As for the religion, they were all Jamdali.

"That's a challenge with human terrain teams," observed Alex. "They have some terrific anthropologists and sociologists, but many of them have a hard time translating their insights into practical application for us. You will either need to do it for them or get them involved to a point where they can make their knowledge meaningful to you.

"So, the representativeness of the Mirgul council is something we should investigate," continued Alex. "It might also be worthwhile at some point to examine religious differences. How about the women?"

We were getting pretty specific requirements from the embassy to get women involved in the government and local councils. I got a lot of expected resistance at first, then some lip service, but I got compliance only when I started to link development money to women's participation on the council. They seemed to perform a perfunctory role, but that should grow over time now that they had their foot in the door.

"What about the corruption issue?" Alex asked.

"Every government official is corrupt," I explained, "and probably most of the town council as well. It is just endemic to the culture. Everyone pays bribes to get things done. I didn't think addressing petty corruption was my job."

Alex continued with the theme. "Do you know how the people here define corruption?"

"I assume it's the standard definition of using official position for private gain."

"I'm sure that is a part of it," said Alex, "but let's think about how they govern themselves and see if we can come up with a better sense of how they think about the issue. Let's move on to development. What was your strategy with that?"

I recognized that giving people jobs and improving their communities was important. We had to compete with Bala Khan and the insurgency for the support of the fighting-age youth. Jobs were one way to do that. If we could also show that we and the government could bring prosperity, then we should be able to gain the support of the communities. We needed to show them the benefits of working with us.

"We determined what projects we thought the people in the local area needed—a better and wider road, schools, electricity, easier access to water, and so on. We hired contractors to do the job," I said.

Alex leaned forward. "How did you determine what people needed?"

"We used a doctrinal assessment tool. Most of the needs were pretty obvious."

"Do you know how many people from the local area were employed in the projects?"

I didn't know. I guessed several hundred, maybe over a thousand, were employed. When I added up all of the positions on the various projects, the total was over a thousand, but I had not actually counted the workers.

Alex pressed the issue further. "Did you see a lot of people at work on the jobs when you passed by the projects?"

No, I hadn't. It did seem like very few people were at work on each of them, mostly outsiders from Ashrabad, but I figured the contractor was managing all of that to get the job done.

"Who owned the projects?"

"The contractor did."

"What are the contractor's incentives?" Asked Alex.

"Profit, of course. Get the job done at the least cost in time, material, and labor."

"Who held the contractor accountable to get the job done right?"

"Well, if they wanted to build a reputation for good work, then they would hold themselves accountable. The governor and I provided oversight."

Alex pressed the point, "How well did that work out?"

"I'm not sure. The Mirgul school collapsed under the earthquake and the canal was destroyed by a rainstorm. Not much we could do about that, although the death of the children was very tragic. The other projects were damaged by the insurgents, so I could not get a good assessment of quality. Besides, there is no way I could inspect every project. My unit lacked the expertise, for one thing. Also, if the work was poor, we would just not hire that business again. They had plenty of motives to do the work properly."

"How many other buildings near the Mirgul school collapsed from the earthquake?"

I did not recall that any other buildings had collapsed.

Alex widened the scope of the discussion. "Who attacked your development projects and why did they attack them?"

"The insurgents attacked them—most likely under Bala Khan's orders. They could not afford to have the government be seen by the people as helping them. One way to undermine legitimacy is to show the people that the government cannot protect the key facilities that support the people."

"You are right about the legitimacy issue, but how certain are you that it was the insurgents who attacked the projects?" Alex asked with a wry smile.

"Of course it was the Jammers, Alex—who else would do that?" retorted Mick. "They have the guns, they have enough money. You are never going to get anything built until you kill or capture enough insurgents that they lack the manpower to carry out attacks. This is why security needs to come first. Governance and development cannot move forward unless you have security. I'm not sure why we took the gloves off and went down this 'hearts and minds' road."

Mick was trying a different argument to get me back into the kinetic operations. What he said seemed to make sense. We had killed scores of insurgents in this scenario, but as in the other ones, the insurgents kept regenerating capacity.

"You are right, Mick, we need to reduce the number of active insurgents." Alex explained. "I am also very skeptical of a pure 'hearts and minds' approach. I think it is misguided."

"Finally, something we can agree on!" cried Mick. "Let's get the readout."

Alex went back up to check on the report. Mick and I went down to a briefing room to talk.

Mick grabbed my shoulders and looked me in the eye. "Well, you tried the softer approach, and it didn't work. We need to get back to targeting the insurgent forces. Once you knock them back, then the other stuff has a chance to be successful."

I was really confused and frustrated. I had tried Mick's approach before and it had not worked—in fact, it made things much worse. There was no way I could simply "follow up" with governance and development in that kind of situation. But the approach in the old COIN manual did not seem to work either. The situation was not as bad, but it was still much worse than it should have been. I was missing something and could not figure out what that was.

"You have to get Bala Khan," said Mick. "He is the key to the whole insurgency. Eliminate him, and you will win."

The techs were ready with the readout, so we went back up to hear the outcome.

Feedback Session

I was really interested in this session—even more so than in the others. We had faced plenty of challenges in Iraq and Afghanistan, even after the manual was published. There were many people who did not buy into the doctrine. Mick was certainly one of those who rejected it outright, even though he was savvy enough to talk the talk. He accepted that governance and development were important, but believed that they needed to come after you eliminated the insurgency . . . something he admittedly never quite managed to do.

Alex was characteristically skeptical about the doctrine. It had the right basic foundation, which is what doctrine needed, but lacked sufficient depth for application in the real world. He also felt it contained some problematic assumptions, which I was sure we would address at some point.

We examined the readout together.

The occupation of the Mirgul base and two observation posts concerned the population but did not enrage them as the previous locations had done. After some initial fighting, the violence moved to the countryside.

The new positions did not affect the aquifers or significant arable land, but the people were worried about the new positions bringing violence to the town. To this point, violence was in the countryside rather than among the people. They were worried you would use the outpost to launch attacks on the village.

Once Bala Khan and his subordinates determined that further efforts to dislodge you would do more harm to the population than good, he directed the attacks to move outside the populated areas. This effort pleased the people—from their standpoint, violence in villages was a violation of common decency. The migration of violence to the countryside also kept your focus out there and away from the villages. This supported Bala Khan's efforts to increase his control of the population. So, moving the violence to the countryside had the effect he intended.

The people did not support the development projects. They were highly upset that the contractors built faulty facilities and failed to employ local people. Bar Pak and the contractors, they were convinced, stole most of the money and left them with projects that were not needed, upset their livelihoods, or did not work.

"I knew they were ungrateful insurgent-breeders. They need to be crushed first, intimidated, and then they will be more supportive."

"Mick, cost-benefit calculus is something we will need to discuss. Let's hold that thought and get the rest of the readout."

Most of the attacks on the development projects were locally inspired rather than the result of insurgent operations. The insurgent leaders were concerned initially about the projects, but when they saw the effects on the people, they decided to let the people deal with the matter. The insurgent leaders focused mainly on pointing out the flaws in the projects and used public outrage to sustain manpower for their attacks on the government and coalition.

For instance, the road-widening project angered the people who lived nearby. They depend on the farmland for livelihood. Adding five meters of width on either side of the road took arable land away from them. Neither the contractor nor the governor offered any compensation for the lost land. In fact, when people sought out the governor to complain, he told them there was nothing he could do about it. He also advised them not to complain to the coalition, because they would put the complainers in jail. Thinking they had no other option, the people began attacking the road workers and planting IEDs. Bala Khan gave them some resources in support, but the attacks were a local affair. Eventually, they succeeded in intimidating the workers and stopping the construction.

The Nangul pipe scheme was destroyed by the people of Fargul. Water from the mountain spring had been regulated for decades under an agreement between the villages of Fargul, Nangul, and Sudgul. The pipe scheme was unregulated and serviced only Nangul and Sudgul, even though the pipes themselves went right past Fargul. Fargul's water supply was now in jeopardy, and that is why the fight broke out at the ribbon-cutting ceremony. The governor also told them not to complain or they would be arrested. The pipe scheme was poorly built and stopped working after two days. The people of Fargul destroyed it afterwards.

The school between Fargul and Sudgul was attacked by militants from both villages. Both villages wanted a school for their children. However, these villages had been feuding for decades over water supply and other issues. They managed to regulate the water dispute, but still held a lot of animosity over land and other issues. They both felt screwed by the school. Only outsiders did the work, so they felt economically disenfranchised. They believed the construction was unsafe. They refused to send their kids to a consolidated school.

In what might be one of the few examples of coordination between the villages since the water agreement, militants from each village took *turns vandalizing the school to ensure no one used it. The militants would take pictures of the damage for Bala Khan and other insurgent leaders to prove they had done the attack. The insurgent leaders would replenish their resources so the attacks could continue.*

The Hamrok well was damaged not by the insurgents but by the women in the village. The well certainly made getting water more convenient—the women did not have to walk two kilometers to the spring—but the women valued that time together away from the village and away from the men. Fetching water gave them the opportunity to talk, counsel, and support one another and to forget their daily toil. The time away was so valuable to the women that they conspired to damage the well. Of course, you got the blame for a poorly thought-out and constructed project.

The Mirgul micro-hydro plant was shoddily built. The contractors fudged the cement mixture on the canal. They knew it would last only a few weeks before it collapsed. They did get their letter of support signed by you and Bar Pak for "quality work," which they will show to other coalition members and government officials. The people of Mirgul were very excited about the project. They did want electricity. Expectations had been raised. They were all the more angry when the canal collapsed and the lights went out again.

The Mirgul school was the biggest calamity of all. The locals were soon aware of the cement mixture being fudged again and worried about the soundness of the structure. That is why only a handful of poor families let their children go to that school. They had no alternative and decided to take their chances. When the school collapsed during the earthquake—notice that no other local structures collapsed—the people were outraged. They figured that you must have been behind the faulty construction. After all, the school was very close to the base. To them, you either wanted the school to collapse and kill the children or did not care enough about them to make sure that something built right under your nose was done right. Either explanation is bad.

These projects were part of the reason your "information operations" efforts rang hollow. People saw the so-called prosperity you promised to be a sham. They were also incensed about how your soldiers acted. They drove at high rates of speed through the bazaar, kicking up dust, which spoiled the meat and fruits and vegetables in the stores. A number of fruit and vegetable carts were knocked over. Two children were killed and four run over by your vehicles. So were two donkeys. The dust was so bad that your drivers probably never saw them—and maybe they did not even know they hit the children and animals. But to the locals, it was another example of careless disregard for the people.

They also hated the visits by the governor. Your soldiers would shout at the people and point their guns at them. This was all done in the name of security for the governor, but the people felt they were being threatened and harassed. The high-handed treatment, they believed, was yet another example of disrespect.

The governor grew to be even more despised by the people. He assembled a group of supporters that he installed as the town council. The members of this "crony council," as it was called, were all from the Merk clan of the Mir. The Merk are a minority group who angled to use their access to the governor and to you to increase their power and authority.

The governor hired his friends as contractors. He would get twenty to twenty-five percent of the money on every contract, and the crony council got a cut as well. The contractor would take twenty to twenty-five percent himself and hire a subcontractor. That subcontractor would take a percentage of the cost. Sometimes these projects were subcontracted three or four times. By the time the money got to the guy who would actually do the work, only fifteen to twenty percent of it was left. So the job manager had to cut back on labor and fudge the cement mixture and use bad wood and materials in order to build the façade of a facility. That is why the projects broke so quickly. For the contractors, the project needed to last only long enough for them to get their final payment, and perhaps a letter from you and the governor. They did not care if it broke. And when it did break, Bar Pak promised that the original contractor would get the repair project, a sort of "planned obsolescence" scheme.

There were other problems with the projects. The job manager was generally nonlocal and brought in outside labor from his area—people there needed jobs as well. Only a few locals were employed on each project, and they were all related to the crony-council. The irrigation ditches and water control points were all placed on council members' land. This gave the council control of a precious resource—and resource control is power. This also fueled resentment.

The people saw you as directly enabling Bar Pak's corruption. When you would cart him from place to place, provide his security, and uncritically support everything he did, the people saw you as part of the problem. You were seen as a well-armed, thousand-man insurance policy for Bar Pak's corruption and abuse of power. You protected him from any accountability. They figured either you were a participant in the scam or you were too stupid to recognize that Bar Pak and the crony council were taking you to the cleaners. Regardless of which explanation they believed, you lost all respect among the people.

Your position was further undermined by your requirement for women on the town council before any project money would be allocated. The people viewed this effort as an outsider dictating a serious social change and holding projects hostage. If you could force them to put women on the town council, what would you dictate next? The people were clearly not ready for the change, especially if directed by an outsider. Their resistance to the idea—and to you—increased.

Bala Khan had to do very little to maintain the support of the people. He just pointed out all of these problems and let people decide for themselves. It was not a difficult choice. "Never interrupt your enemy while he is destroying himself," Bala Khan would say. He kept up some perfunctory attacks on your positions just to maintain credibility and to keep you away from the people while his influence efforts were at work. Behind the scenes, his popular support was growing.

Bala Khan quoted Napoleon; that was interesting. Even more interesting, and troubling, was the fact that even though I followed the old COIN manual, my efforts still fell victim to the law of unintended consequences. I was beginning to think that defeating a local insurgency was impossible. We tried kinetic operations, we tried comprehensive COIN. Nothing seemed to work.

"This was a bit like the boiling frog syndrome," Alex began. "You did not get the violent reaction from the population, as in the first two scenarios. This time local support eroded over time."

"Boiling frog?"

"Allegedly—I've never tried it myself—if you put a frog into a pot of boiling water, it will jump out immediately. If, however, you put it into room temperature water and slowly turn up the heat, the frog will simply fall asleep and boil to death. In some respects, our efforts this time created a slow boil among the population, generating more and more support for Bala Khan and the insurgency. We were dying a slow death. Why do you think that happened?"

Mick interrupted, "Because these backward people have no idea what is good for them. They are ungrateful, corrupt, and stupid. That's why this happened, and that's why we need to teach them hard lessons rather than coddling them with a sissy hearts and minds approach. Trying to bring a fifteenth-century society into the twenty-first century in a year is foolish. Let them have their Middle Ages, like we did."

I sensed that Mick was beginning to come unglued. The simulation seemed to place even more stress on him than it did on me. He was trying to justify an approach that clearly did not work in this exercise but seemed to have become an article of faith to him.

"We will get to hearts and minds a bit later," said Alex. "What is your assessment of this outcome?"

I said I was frustrated and really confused. I recognized the purely kinetic approach was ineffective. We seemed to kill or capture nearly as many insurgents using comprehensive COIN as we did with the kinetic approach, and with fewer casualties on our side, which was good news. The population did not react violently to our presence immediately, but their anger clearly grew over time. We had done better, but not nearly well enough. It seemed as though our Achilles heel was the government. As long as it was corrupt and incompetent, we would never get the population on our side. Were we engaged in a hopeless mission?

"Weak governance—lack of capacity and incompetence—and bad governance—corruption and abuse of power—are core problems that need to be addressed to be successful. We can influence some of that. Let's begin with the heart of the matter: the people. What was your strategy for influencing them?" asked Alex.

"I wanted to limit the downside effects of our presence by being more careful in selecting our positions and limiting civilian casualties. Clearly some of our tactical practices still alienated them. I also wanted to use development to increase prosperity. If they saw the benefits of working together with us, they would make the choice to do so over time. So we made an assessment of what the people needed and what would bring them prosperity and got the projects lined up. I had no idea what Bar Pak and his cronies were doing with the money. I can see how the people would be upset. And forcing them to put women on the council put them over the edge."

Alex began, "Let's start with the assessment of what people needed. Who made that assessment?"

"I did, with some consultation with Bar Pak."

"How did the people feel about all this?" asked Alex.

"I didn't know at the time. Given their reaction to some of the projects, it seemed that they were not too enthusiastic."

"Bar Pak is the governor," interjected Mick. "He is the representative of the people and should know what they need. We did nothing wrong here. This is Bar Pak's fault."

"Is he really the representative of the people?" asked Alex. "How did Bar Pak become the governor?"

"He was appointed by the central government. They do not have elections for governor. They have always done it this way," I replied.

"True enough," said Alex. "But in former days, governors had to figure out how to gain enough popular support for their policies. Otherwise, the people would revolt. There are plenty of historical examples of that as well. Unlike Bar Pak, those governors did not have a battalion of Americans to protect them."

"So we insulated Bar Pak from public accountability. As long as we were around, Bar Pak could act with impunity. If the people tried to revolt, we would simply put it down in the name of counterinsurgency."

"Well, insurgency is a form of popular revolt," noted Alex. "But you are correct, there is no public accountability in the system right now."

He was right. The people couldn't impeach him, they couldn't elect someone else, and there was no credible ombudsman to take and act on complaints. They obviously felt they couldn't come to us either.

"Then they should tell us!" yelled Mick. "How else are we supposed to know?"

"That was part of the problem," I said. "The people believed that we were backing the governor—maybe even complicit in his abuse of power. He even told them not to raise complaints about the road-widening project with us because we would throw them in jail. Bar Pak was using us as his bouncers to avoid accountability, enrich himself and his friends, and stay in power. We had no credibility with the people." I was sickened.

"So we have to figure out some way to promote public accountability," Alex suggested.

Power corrupts. Absolute power corrupts absolutely. We needed to work ourselves into the position as an honest broker with our resources and capabilities.

"We are also supposed to be supporting the government," said Mick. "You can't have it both ways."

Mick had a point. On the one hand, we were supposed to support the government. On the other, we needed to avoid enabling abuse of power.

"Let's be careful of creating false choices," observed Alex. "We need to promote legitimate and credible government *and* governance. That does not mean simply offering uncritical support to particular officials. By unintentionally enabling abuse of power, we are actually undermining legitimacy and credibility. Now here is where the difference between official government and governance comes into play. Historically, how did governors coordinate with the people?"

"They worked with the councils," I replied. "The councils represented the people, the governor represented the government. That is how they made decisions and solved problems. Governance here is viewed as balanced interaction between officials and traditional councils to build consensus, make decisions, solve problems, and promote accountability. The local voice is what has been missing.

"The crony council was just a façade. They represented only a single social group within the tribe. The Merk were superempowered, and the others were left out. The perception of unfairness and social exclusion was the main issue behind corruption and abuse of power. Naseem tried to warn me about this, but I didn't listen."

"Excellent. Now with that in mind, let's discuss development." Alex took a deep breath. "Tell me, have you ever changed the oil on a rental car?"

"What kind of silly question is that?" Mick was growing more impatient.

But I got the point immediately. We don't change the oil in a rental car because we feel no sense of ownership. Maintaining the car is someone else's problem. We take care of our own cars because we paid for them with our work and sweat; we own them, and we want them to last.

The people had absolutely no ownership in the development projects. Bar Pak and I figured out what was good for the people, without bothering to ask them. We brought in outsiders to build things people did not want or need. They got very few jobs out of the effort, and because of corruption, the facilities themselves were poorly constructed—with deadly consequences in at least one case. They got nothing from it but crap.

"The people here have a great saying: 'If you sweat for it, you protect it.' Have you ever read Greg Mortenson's books, *Three Cups of Tea* and *Stones into Schools?*" asked Alex.

I had read them, but now the key lessons were starting to come clear. Greg emphasized "sweat equity" in all his schools. The people had to want the school, and were required to donate the land and a portion of the labor and materials. This was the community's school, not Greg's. His schools were always protected by the community—they simply did not get attacked or vandalized. The people sweated for it, they protected it.

We failed the ownership and sweat equity tests. The people had no say. We built what we wanted and what we thought they needed. These were our projects, not theirs, and we did not cover ourselves in glory with quality. We gave them a bad rental car they did not need and then we wondered why they did not change the oil in it.

"Spare the rod, spoil the child," Mick interjected. "So, Alex, do you see this as some social engineering experiment? Just give people what they want and a miracle occurs and they stop being insurgents? There was a great saying in Vietnam—if you have them by the balls, their hearts and minds will follow. We need more of that."

"Well, I'm not so sure the method worked too well in Vietnam either," Alex noted. "But we should take on this hearts and minds issue that keeps coming up. What do you think about that?"

A part of me saw the logic in hearts and minds. If you win the people over to your side, then you will defeat the insurgency. But the win-with-kindness approach seemed pretty glib and unrealistic. The people could simply take advantage of the kindness and betray us. And unless the government proved itself worthy of popular support, any short-terms gains from hearts and minds would be fleeting. The opposite approach of just focusing on chasing and killing insurgents had proven itself flawed as well. I was sure there was a logical position between the extremes, but I was having a hard time finding it.

Alex sat back in his chair. "Let's start by thinking about it in terms of basic economics—supply and demand. Supply is the available pool of insurgents and potential fighters. Demand is the signal from the population for insurgent activity, or at least acquiescence in it. The two have a symbiotic relationship—as the demand signal increases from the population, the supply must respond. If the signal for demand is stronger than the available supply, more supply is created. Which side of the equation are you working?"

"As you define it," I said, "we are more focused on the supply side. If we can kill or capture enough insurgents, and use projects to keep young men employed, then we can reduce the available supply of insurgents. As the available supply goes to zero, then the insurgency grows weaker and is defeated."

"What do you know about the demographics, the potential supply?" inquired Alex.

"Over seventy percent of the population is under the age of twenty-five. There are tens of thousands of potential insurgents. As Petraeus says, as long as they have reasons for fighting, we will not kill our way out of the insurgency."

"Good. So the attrition model—the supply-side approach alone—is a practical impossibility," Alex noted.

"That's right," I affirmed. "As long as they have reasons for fighting and a willingness and capability to fight, we are likely to get nowhere through an attrition model."

"Of course," Alex suggested, "eliminating critical capability to continue fighting—eliminating sanctuary, closing off all supplies, isolating them from the population—could make an attrition model successful."

"But we don't have the ability to do that here," I pointed out. "Sanctuary in Markhand, the porous border and mountainous terrain, the widespread support of the population, the weak and bad governance, and the simple lack of forces to geographically isolate the insurgent forces all make that approach unfeasible here."

"Correct," said Alex. "So we also need to take a look at the demand side of the equation—addressing the issues that affect the demand for insurgents in the first place. By reducing the demand signal indirectly, we affect the supply. So how do we do that?"

"Most insurgents, at least in this area, appear to fight for very practical reasons. Some fight for money—to put food on the table or for personal gain. Others have grievances or problems with the government, with us, or with a neighboring tribe. Others believe they are defending their homes and villages. Of course, most fight for a combination of these reasons. Addressing those issues can reduce the reasons for supporting insurgency in the first place."

"So now we are back to soldiers-as-social-workers running local affairs—more hearts and minds crap—is that right, Alex?" snorted Mick.

"Not entirely," Alex replied. "That would put us in the position of governing, which we lack the competence and knowledge to do. I'm thinking of something a bit more cold blooded. Now before we move on, there are also the hardcore ideologues and those hungry for personal power. They are likely to keep fighting no matter what."

"Yes," I agreed, "but we really do not know who is who—right now they are joined together. We have to find some way of splitting them apart so the lunatics are isolated from the rest."

"Right," said Alex, "so the demand-side of the equation has limitations as well. Finding the right balance of effort is critical. Getting at the supply side is pretty straightforward but takes us nowhere unless we affect the demand side—we have to target the sources of their strength, not just their forces."

"But this leads us back to Mick's point about being social workers, judges, governors, and so on—which we are not capable of doing."

"Correct," Alex replied. "The people and the government have to do that themselves. The most effective form of counterinsurgency, and of insurgency, for that matter, is grassroots political and social mobilization. The people are actors in this environment, not simply individuals being acted upon. Insurgents understand this . . . and so do effective politicians. They learn to get the people working on a common agenda."

Mick shook his head. "So now soldiers have to be politicians, too?"

"No," I interjected, "we can't do that, as outsiders. We have to influence popular mobilization. But doesn't that put us right back to the problem of governance and government? People are not going to mobilize in support of something they find repulsive, and that's the current state of government."

"Exactly," Alex reassured me. "Do you recall the advice Naseem kept giving you?"

"You mean about local ownership and public accountability?"

Alex nodded. "He said he wanted to get the people to own the problems and the solutions, whether projects and economic development, role in governance through representative councils that check and balance the official government, or means of raising and redressing complaints and grievances."

I got that in concept; I also got that Bar Pak and other officials had way too much stake in the current system that combines personal power with little to no public accountability. But until the government reformed itself, we were stuck with this problem.

"Looks like we are back to the supply side of things after all," said Mick. "We need to kill enough of them, grind off the insurgents well enough, and build the security forces so we can hand over the fight to the KNA and KNP. Governance is their problem, not ours. If they want to have a perpetual insurgency on their hands because they are too f—ed up to fix themselves, then that is their problem, not ours."

"But it is our problem as long as we are here and our soldiers are in the fight," said Alex. "But you both make the point that our demand-side efforts will only be successful to a certain point—the central government will need to solve their problems for any local solutions to be lasting."

"But we can affect the local environment and we can facilitate local solutions that undermine the local insurgency," Alex continued. "We cannot force people to actively support their government, but we can help promote popular intolerance against insurgent violence. Once people view the insurgents as the greater threat, the tables can turn against them very quickly. That's what I mean by targeting the demand-side of the equation—undermining the sources of the insurgents' strength."

I said I was all for that but had no idea how to start.

"Have you ever read any studies on behavioral economics?" asked Alex.

"I haven't. I've heard people talk about a book called *Freakonomics* but it just seemed like flaky pseudoscience to me."

"You are right to be skeptical, but informed skepticism is the key. The basic point behind behavioral economics is that people respond to incentives."

"Sounds like another silly argument for buying support," retorted Mick.

"Well, incentives can be positive or negative—carrots and sticks—if you will," explained Alex. "This gets back to the issue of cost-benefit calculations that we touched upon earlier. The trick is to design the incentive structures in a way that are meaningful to people. The costs and the benefits have to be compelling from their perspective. That means you have to know enough about the society, local politics, and economics to understand how to use your resources and capabilities to design the incentives."

"I thought I tried this earlier—provide benefits to those supporting us, inflict costs on those against us—but the approach didn't seem to work very well."

"Perhaps what seemed like important costs and benefits from our perspective were not seen by the people as particularly compelling," noted Alex.

Alex was right, we had mirror-imaged what we thought might be important onto the population. We needed to determine what was compelling in their eyes.

Mick threw up his hands. "That would take decades of study—it's completely unrealistic."

"Possibly," said Alex, "but we can take a lot of hints from the society to accelerate the learning process. We do not need to do this on our own if we get the people involved. That's why governance is more important than government. Effective governance can help us design the incentives. We will need to learn and adapt quickly—it will take some trial and error to get things close enough to being compelling that behavior and choices begin to change."

Fascinating. I had not thought about counterinsurgency in this way before. "I think this is what General McChrystal meant when he said counterinsurgency is an argument for the support of the people. The side that affects the cost-benefit calculations more effectively has a distinct advantage. Up to this point, the people saw only the very high cost and low benefits of working with us and the government. Violence was a high cost; so were civilian casualties and deaths of fighters; so were corruption, abuse of power, and social marginalization of those outside Bar Pak's small circle of cronies. Collapsing schools, projects that did not work or were unwanted, even how we treated the people in the markets were all compelling costs in the eyes of the people. Only Bar Pak, Al'a Dust, and a small circle of favorites had any compelling benefits from our presence.

"All that Bala Khan and the insurgent leaders had to do to win the argument was point to these problems as costs to society and the people," I continued, "and show themselves as protectors against us and against a predatory government. We raised the costs of supporting us while lowering the benefits. Bala Khan raised the benefits of supporting him while lowering the relative costs. And we made it easy for him."

I picked up on something Alex said earlier as well. "We don't necessarily need people to actively support the government right away. We just need them to actively oppose insurgent violence. Getting them actively engaged in governance so they can work on resolving issues of compelling importance to them is the critical first step. Certainly we will keep fighting the insurgents—dealing with the supply side of the equation. But targeting the demand side is even more important. The people need to be actors in stability. They will isolate the ones opposed, undermining the insurgents' ability to regenerate and making them more vulnerable. Other issues will be solved much more easily in a relatively stable environment."

"At the end of the day, counterinsurgency is pretty cold blooded," Alex explained. "You are trying to win the argument for the support of the people. It is not a popularity contest, it is a matter of affecting the cost-benefit equation in our favor. If they wind up liking you in the process, so much the better. But what we are really trying to understand is how people make choices for themselves and their communities out of self-interest. We want to shape those interests to align with our interests of stability and defeating the insurgency. Naseem seems to understand this pretty well. So where do we go from here?"

I needed to do some reading, and some thinking. I left the simulator and walked up the stairs into the daylight for some fresh air and fresh thinking. I felt a sort of mental click, kind of like the sound and feel of a lock opening when the combination is right. So many "truths" that I believed in—had been trained and convinced to believe in—were turning out to be wrong. Those mentalities had consistently led me down the wrong paths and into dead ends.

For the first time in my career, I felt that I was getting an education. I was beginning to understand why counterinsurgency is more than just killing or capturing insurgents, and why doctrine provided a common professional language but not a recipe for success. I had to determine a unique solution—or set of solutions—to a very unique situation. But I also had to learn and adapt as the situation evolved. I had to think and act differently.

I would also have to get my soldiers to think and act differently. It was not enough for me to hold a set of ideas in my head if my soldiers did not understand them and act upon them. I needed to win the argument for their support as well. My chain of command would also be a challenge. They were raised and trained in the same mindset as I had been. Operating differently would generate a lot of pushback from them if I could not convince them what I was doing was right. I would need to weather the storm and stick to my guns, even if that cost me personally.

Getting back to Mirgul, I needed to start with what the people knew and how they governed themselves. I had to help get a properly consti-tuted council in place but needed to do so in a way that made it their ini-tiative and not mine. They needed to own everything, which meant they would need to sweat for everything as well. I needed to get them to place their honor on the line. Through their ownership, they would help me design the incentive structure.

Defeating a local insurgency first involved changing cost-benefit cal-culations among the people in favor of stability—changing the demand side of the equation. They might not ever like us or want us to be there over the long term, and they might not welcome the government with open arms, but they wanted to be able to go about the business of normal, everyday life. Violence and unnecessary disruption militated against that.

We also needed to demonstrate tangible and compelling benefits of our presence—compelling in the eyes of the people. We needed the people to convince themselves that the insurgents were the ones disrupting their lives and preventing people and communities from reaching their needs and desires. We needed to turn the tables on the cost-benefit equation.

Next, we needed people to take active measures to promote stability and marginalize the insurgents. Once the people were convinced that working together for stability and "normalcy" was more compelling than providing active or even passive support to the insurgency, then the people's intolerance of violence would increase. We had to figure out ways to use our "carrots" as "sticks"—to show the people that they would lose compelling opportunities for their communities if violence continued. The insurgents would be marginalized and isolated from their communities once popular intolerance for their violence grew strong enough.

Once the insurgents were isolated from the population, then we could target them to lasting effect. When the insurgents had popular control or support, they regenerated combat power just as quickly as we could degrade it—or even more quickly. We needed to get COIN math working in our favor. Once insurgents were fighting and losing for a cause no one supported any longer, then they would be fatally undermined.

At the same time, I needed to determine ways to hold Bar Pak and the government accountable. I needed to shift my focus from supporting government officials to supporting credible and legitimate governance. That involved both the official government and the local councils. We needed to help them create sufficient checks and balances so corruption and abuse of power would be curtailed and the needs of the people would be discussed and met. I needed to be seen as on the side of the people and stability and legitimacy—and to take action against anyone or anything that threatened them.

Those were the general principles. I would need to adapt to each situation and make the necessary adjustments over time as the dynamics evolved.

I met Alex outside a few hours later and explained my vision. I was seeing the fight from a very different perspective than I had beforehand. I had him to thank for it.

"All I did was ask a few leading questions. You figured this out on your own once you opened your mind to other approaches."

"I was never very good at thinking outside the box. I can execute doctrine and tactics, techniques and procedures really well. But thinking differently and beyond conventional wisdom has never been a strength for me."

Alex continued, "I'm not sure anyone truly thinks 'outside the box.' We build mental models for ourselves through our own experiences and those of others, through history, and through theory. We apply those mental models to various situations. I have always tried to expand my box—

expand my mental models. The more we do so, the more often we might think outside someone else's box—which can create some challenges within the organization—but our own box is something we define for ourselves."

"How do you expand your box?"

"Personal experience is critical," Alex replied, "but even the most fortunate can have only so much. So learning from the experiences of others is important as well. I've always supplemented that by reading history; not just military history, but other historical disciplines as well: social, political, economic, cultural. Theory is also important in helping to construct and challenge mental models. Clausewitz and Sun Tzu are classics. I have found that drawing from other subjects such as psychology, economics, behavioral economics, chaos and complexity, and sociology has enabled me to think differently about the challenges we face."

"And the larger and deeper our mental models become, the better we learn and adapt."

"You are right about the learning and adaptation. This is going to be incredibly complex. Think about it. In the simple game of chess—two sides, sixteen pieces each, an eight-by-eight board, both people playing by the same rules—the number of possible combinations of moves over the course of the game is 10 to the 120th power.

"Here you have multisided, multidimensional chess. You are a side; so are the government, the police, the KNA, the councils, the businessmen, the insurgents, the religious leaders. That alone is eight sides. You all play by different rules, and those rules change, and you do not always know what rules the others are using. You also do not see the entire board. You only see what is in front of you or what people choose to let you see—which might be accurate or misleading."

"How do you prepare for that?" I asked. "How do you deal with it?"

"I'm not sure one can ever be fully prepared for that kind of complexity. It is hard enough understanding our own society, and here we are dealing with a culture and society very different from our own. The capacity to learn and adapt is important, but you also have to remember that the other sides are learning and adapting as well.

"We sometimes forget that we are not simply acting upon a static environment," Alex continued. "I've seen plenty of examples of organizations learning and making an adaptation but then failing to account for the adaptations of others. They persist in a single change to the mental model, thinking they have everything figured out. But this is a dynamically complex environment. You have to sense the adaptations of others and understand how the dynamics of the conflict are changing so you can continue making the necessary adjustments."

"That's going to be pretty chaotic." I was having a hard time understanding how anyone could possibly manage all of this—and explain it to our soldiers so they can stay on the same page.

"This is where chaos and complexity theories can come in handy. You are going to experience some interactions that are linear—they have simple and proportional cause and effect. A sniper fires a bullet and kills an insurgent, for example. You will also experience interactions that are nonlinear—they defy simple and proportional cause and effect. The first outpost near Mirgul is a good example. The seemingly simple act of emplacing the position where you did caused nonlinear reactions that you could not anticipate given your mental model and understanding of the environment. That's part of the challenge—you cannot reasonably anticipate all of the outcomes of your actions."

"I'm not feeling much better about all of this," I confessed. "I'm only starting to understand it—explaining it in simple language to a thousand-member organization seems impossible."

"What the theories also suggest, to me at least, is that the best way to shape the outcomes is by influencing the rules that govern the interactions. For instance, the simulation you are in now is actually governed by a few simple rules for each actor. The interactions of many people operating under a simple set of rules create complex, dynamic outcomes. Right now, your soldiers operate by rules that almost exclusively emphasize force protection and insurgent targeting. That is part of the reason why cutting down farmers' pomegranate trees to build the outpost was perfectly rational to them."

"So I need to alter the rules by which my soldiers operate so they are aligned with the new approach."

"Precisely. The side with the dominant strategy is best able to determine the outcomes, and the rules enable you to implement the strategy consistently. The dominant strategy is the one that has the most compelling effect on the cost-benefit calculations of the others. The other actors have to adapt to it.

"The one you outlined earlier is a good start: Win the argument for the support of the people by demonstrating to them that they can best meet the needs of their communities by working together for stability. They must believe they own the outcome. As they become convinced of this, their intolerance for those who disrupt their efforts will grow. If they are convinced they can take action while remaining safe, they are likely to begin working against the insurgents. Their sense of security is critically important here. Once the insurgents are marginalized and isolated from the population, then your kinetic operations will have lasting effects. When the insurgents have lost popular support and are unable to regenerate combat power, they are fatally undermined and on the clear path toward defeat.

"Winning the argument for the support of the people, therefore, does not mean you are trying to win a 'hearts and minds' popularity contest—that is a very dangerous concept. You want to shape behavioral outcomes so you can defeat the insurgency. People might like you, but if there is still a raging local insurgency, then you have failed."

I understood the logic completely. We needed to shape, influence, manipulate the cost-benefit calculations of the various actors. We had a variety of capabilities to affect those calculations. Security, governance, development, information, and personal relationships were categories to think through in developing the levers. Insurgency is a sociopolitical phenomenon. We wanted to create an environment in which the people took an active role in defeating the insurgency—in which they mobilized. Once social intolerance for insurgency was created and people marginalized and isolated the insurgents, then we could kill or capture them and they would not regenerate locally. That was how to defeat them.

"But how do I keep a thousand soldiers on the same page? Clearly we can have the dominant strategy, but if our soldiers and junior leaders are on a different wavelength, their individual actions could actually work against what we are trying to do. Chopping down the pomegranate trees for our first outpost, for instance, was a sound tactical action that helped turn people against us."

"How do you communicate your intent and methods to them now?"

"In garrison, we have a lot of venues—formations, meetings, leader development, and so on. In the field, I can do so on battlefield circulation to our various positions. But I clearly need to do more than just inspect fighting positions and see how people are doing. I need to use every moment with them to communicate my intent and concept of operations and how we are going to win. I also need the battalion chain of command down to the junior team leaders working this for me. Every soldier needs to own the car."

"Exactly right. In counterinsurgency, our soldiers and junior leaders are making multiple decisions every day that affect the environment and our credibility. I have found that creating some simple rules that everyone understands and that are in line with our intent and concept of operations can serve as a useful guide for decision making and enable a thousand-soldier organization to act with consistency. That makes for a powerful organization.

Alex pulled up a document on his handheld computer. "I used three simple rules."

I looked over the document; it was a handout apparently created for some kind of training session.

"These three simple rules and their brief explanations provided a pretty good guide for decision making. Certainly there are conflicts and ambiguities—no single set is perfect. But I found that soldiers made the right decisions in very difficult and complex situations once they knew what we intended to do and why."

Give people a reason to support the government . . . and you.
- Hold officials and councils and community leaders accountable for good governance.
- Operate in ways that demonstrate respect for the people and their communities.
- Treat people with dignity and respect—how we treat people is combat power.
- Get the people actively involved in stability and actively opposing insurgent violence.

Punish the enemy and take the fun out of insurgency.
- Dominate and win every fight. Losing is no fun for the enemy.
- Be unpredictable. Use different routes, timing, and positions. Make the enemy believe you are watching everywhere, all the time.

- Deploy into the red zone with overwhelming force. An insurgent that does not fight loses credibility.
- Win the argument for the support of the people. Losing every fight for a cause the people do not support will crush insurgent morale.

Locals solve local problems.
- We can provide assistance, but the people need to be responsible and accountable for solving their own problems.
- The people need to own the solutions and the outcome. They will have to live with them long after we are gone.
- When people own solutions they also own the sustainability of those solutions. Use every opportunity to build lasting capacity.
- Maintain our moral, ethical, and legal standards in everything we do. Those are important boundaries for our support.

I decided to use this set of rules as a start and adapt from there. Getting the concept—the dominant strategy—right was essential. The adaptations over time would come within the framework of the strategy. That is how we would maintain consistency at the core and make necessary adjustments as the environment changed. Of course, if the strategy proved wrong, we would need to change it too, but I was fairly certain this was the right path.

I needed to communicate that strategy before deployment and explain why it was the right one to our soldiers—they needed to understand it and own it. The counterinsurgency guidance published by Generals Petraeus and McChrystal back in Iraq and Afghanistan would be a great foundation for creating a common mental model. I also needed to constantly reinforce this during the deployment on every visit. I felt that I would also need to show the effects of what we were doing over time to reinforce that we were on the right track. Progress in counterinsurgency can be slow and difficult to discern on a daily basis. But showing the changes over three or four months' time would be powerful.

Another mental click that I made was the fact that the population was a critical actor. I had always seen them as an entity that was acted upon but not necessarily as an active force in the environment. In fact, the people were the most important actor in the environment. Their ownership as a force for stability would make the difference between success and failure. I needed to get them in the game and aligned with our side.

My Key Lessons

Counterinsurgency is an argument for the support of the people—to favor stability over insurgent violence. They are the critical actors in the environment. They might not like us or the government, but we can work together toward a common goal of stability and supporting the needs of the communities. That is how we can get COIN math to work to our advantage.

"Hearts and minds" can be a dangerous concept. Counterinsurgency is not a popularity contest. It is the cold-blooded application of our resources and capabilities to generate behavioral outcomes, such as social intolerance for insurgency and active measures to marginalize and isolate the insurgents from the people. Once that happens, we can target the isolated groups and defeat them. We can incentivize behaviors; attitudes will change as people see their behaviors creating desired outcomes.

Deliberately manage the cost-benefit equation. Both sides of the ledger need to be compelling enough to generate change in choices and behavior. We need to understand the rules the different actors operate under and what issues are compelling for them. Once we know that, we can apply our resources and capabilities purposefully; we can target the demand side of the equation. Learn and adapt—the environment changes constantly, and we need to adapt our practices to shape choices and behavior effectively.

Local ownership: The people need to own the solutions and the outcomes. If we solve the problem, we create dependency and we become the scapegoat when things go wrong. When people own the outcomes, they will develop ways to ensure the solutions are durable. We need to facilitate ownership and durability. If you sweat for it, you protect it.

Governance trumps government. Mutual accountability and checks and balances are necessary for effective governance. We need to take the side of credibility, legitimacy, and accountability in support of the people. When we take the sides of individuals or specific groups, those people become superempowered and begin to act with impunity. We need to work ourselves into a credible honest broker role in every issue that requires our involvement.

Communicate effectively. Our actions communicate far more powerfully than anything we say or put on a flyer or newsletter. When we say we support the people and then take actions that leave them out of important decision making or fail to treat them with dignity and respect, then we undermine our own credibility. As the Afghans would say, "We hear with our eyes, not just with our ears." How we treat people is combat power for one side or the other. We need to generate the combat power for our side from the people. Our soldiers need to understand what we are doing and, more importantly, why we are doing it. When they "own" the intent and concept of operations, they will make the right decisions.

Putting Theory into Practice

After the conversation with Alex, I did some more reflecting and reading that evening. I returned the next morning and walked down to the simulator, where I met Mick.

I wasn't sure how Mick would have taken my conversation with Alex, and I was glad he hadn't been there. I'd been free to explore some ideas that I would not feel comfortable discussing around Mick. I respected him greatly, but with him I felt limited, trapped in a certain way of thinking. And that way of thinking had led to some bad outcomes that would have cost soldiers' lives in the real world.

He was clearly not happy the last time I tried to go with the original doctrine rather than his methods, which he maintained were an application of the doctrine. I was not looking forward to his response when I explained how I was going to approach this scenario.

I also could not figure out the nature of the relationship between Alex and Mick. The two clearly shared a bond forged in combat. But they could not be more different people. Alex showed tremendous patience and respect, even though Mick did not always reciprocate it. That might have been as much out of consideration for me as it was for Mick.

Alex had a reputation as a brilliant counterinsurgent—a reputation that had grown over time as it became clear what his units had achieved and his own personal impact in turning things around in the wars. That reputation was held back in part because his methods were so different from the norm at the time that he got tremendous pushback from his chain of command. He stuck to his guns at cost to his personal career, but that did not seem to matter to him. Principle was more important than promotion or pleasing superiors.

Mick always characterized Alex as getting the easier tasks, often using his own high casualty rates and number of valor medals his soldiers were awarded to make the case. He even intimated that Alex was not a good warfighter, and that he used the population focus as cover for it. I had believed that for a long time.

Then I found some Center for Army Lessons Learned products about Alex's operations. I found his approach to be inspired. He essentially "maneuvered" by winning the argument within communities and isolating the insurgents into increasingly narrow and isolated geographic locations.

Large-scale operations were shaped beforehand with local support and buy-in. He believed in using deception, unpredictability, and perceptions of overwhelming force to confuse the insurgents and force them into making bad decisions, which he and his soldiers were always ready to capitalize upon. He never wanted his soldiers to be in a position in which their valor alone would determine outcome. These methods required more patience than most others could endure, but they were incredibly effective . . . and devastating for the insurgents.

With the people, he emphasized predictable credibility and local ownership. At the population's request, he supported local, written agreements that established rules and expectations governing how the government officials, security forces, local councils, and his forces would interact. Most of the insurgents simply stopped fighting as a result of social pressure. The ones who continued to fight became more and more isolated. The population turned against them. When they were forced to move to mountain hideouts away from the villages, Alex pounced and annihilated them. The population actually celebrated.

Mick had said this was evidence of a poorly led insurgency—that Alex and his unit faced a dumb and incompetent enemy while the real fight was in Mick's area. Given the high numbers of casualties these insurgents had generated on the coalition previously, I hardly think they were dumb or incompetent—just the opposite. But Alex made them look that way. That's genius in my book.

Making Adjustments

"Ready to have another crack at Bala Khan and his band of lunatics?" Mick smiled as he flexed his biceps.

I told Mick that I was going to try a different application of doctrine, and briefly explained what I intended to do.

Mick shook his head in a combination of disbelief and disgust. "I should have never left you alone with Alex. He's obviously filled your head with a bunch of nonsense. You are a better warfighter than that."

"It's a simulation. The point is that we can try all sorts of different ideas and see what works and what doesn't."

"Never forget that just because something works or doesn't work in a simulation does not mean it will be the same way in the real world. In fact, you might find it to be the opposite."

I agreed that this kind of simulation, as good as it was, was imperfect, but I could not help wondering whether Mick's comment was for my benefit or his own.

I worked with the techs to modify the rules under which my soldiers operated, building our new strategy into their instructions. We rewound the game to just after the Mirgul positions were established.

The focus areas for my staff needed to be retooled. Previously, my intelligence staff had focused exclusively on the enemy. As Alex once remarked, "What you look for tends to be what you see." I now began to understand what he meant by that.

I needed a broader picture of the environment—the social dynamics, the political and economic issues. I also needed to assess how various actors in the environment responded to one another and to us. I needed to gain an understanding of the rules under which they operated so I could anticipate their reactions and adaptations. The staff would require some additional manpower. I also needed to get that capability resident within the companies. All my soldiers had to be scouts, gaining information about the environment on every patrol. They needed to look for more than just the enemy.

We aimed to get COIN math working to our advantage. A savvy counterinsurgent who built ten credible relationships could generate hundreds of allies. Getting the people actively involved was critical.

The intel-to-operations integration had to be changed. In the past, our focus on the insurgent forces had driven our operations. Now, our broader understanding of the environment and the different outcomes we would try to achieve needed to govern operations. Affecting this change was easy in simulation. It would be harder to break the old habits in real life.

Understanding the Environment

I decided to start the approach in Nargul. It was arguably easier—a fairly solid degree of social consensus and cohesion appeared to exist there. Once we showed how we focused on popular ownership and accountability, word would eventually get to Mirgul and the surrounding communities. That could make the more difficult areas a bit more manageable. Plus, it would give us good practice in a more permissive area.

Over the first few weeks, my soldiers interacted with villagers, and my leaders interacted with various counterparts. We created "spheres of influence" for every level. Everyone interacted with people on the street; team and squad leaders interacted with their police and KNA counterparts and local shopkeepers; platoon leaders focused on elders and community leaders and police and KNA counterparts; company leaders focused on community senior leaders and senior police, army, and government officials.

We began to learn a lot about the environment and society and how things worked in the communities. We learned about the four major tribes. The Nar and Mir we had known before. The Zari and the seminomadic Marzin were new to us. We also started to understand the various clan and family structures. I felt like an amateur anthropologist. We asked about the key influencers, but that information was often contradictory. We would need to test who really had credibility and who did not.

I also wanted to understand a bit more about the religion.

"The people of Khanastan are deeply religious," Naseem told me. "They know your soldiers refer to them as 'Jammers' and they deeply resent it. I deeply resent it."

I apologized to Naseem and said that no offense was intended.

"When you disparage our religion, you motivate people to fight even harder. It does not matter that you do not intend any offense. What matters is what they perceive. Right now, people think you are making war on their religion. That does not put you in a good position."

I told Naseem that I would fix this problem within the command. I asked him to teach me about the religion.

"Jamdali is a religion of peace," he began. Naseem told me about their system of beliefs and the main points of Jamdali doctrine.

I asked him if Jamdali had any different sects, noting that Christianity had many.

"Yes, and these are very important. Most of the people follow the moderate Hambali school. They believe that the job of the religious leader is to convey the words of the sacred texts to the people, but the people decide how to interpret and apply the lessons.

"The Takriri follow the Domol school. It is a very radical sect dominated by the religious leaders. They believe the job of the cleric is to interpret the texts and tell people how to apply them. You can see how the religion can get quickly politicized when the cleric tells people what to think. The Domol have set up a host of religious schools in Khanastan and Markhand in which young men get indoctrinated."

"So the Hambalis are moderate; the Domol are more evangelical and politicized."

"Correct. The Nar and Mir are Hambalis; they do not follow the Domol school. The Zari area follows the Jamma Rhun school. It is more moderate than the Domol but still heavily influenced by clerical interpretation. Insurgent leader Sher Wali claims to be Jamma Rhun, but his practices are closer to Domol. This is very important to understand."

"If I understand this correctly, then one of the ways to connect with the Zari and marginalize Sher Wali is through the clerics," I suggested.

"Yes. Do not go overboard with the clerics, but do build relations with them. You have to become real flesh and real blood to the people . . . and they need to become real flesh and real blood to you."

"I don't quite understand what you mean."

"You appear to the people as aliens who descend from an iron box, girded in helmets, body armor, weapons, and sunglasses," he said. "You do not appear human to them. And based on your soldiers' behavior, the people do not believe that they appear human to you.

"It is much easier," Naseem continued, "to take the life of an alien than of a fellow human. The more human you appear to each other, the less cheaply you may regard one another's lives."

I began to trust Naseem's instincts and advice. Our partnership grew quickly. Comrades accept one another as they are; friends change one another. We were beginning to be comrades. I wondered if we would become friends.

I wanted our relationship to serve as a model for the rest of the battalion. We partnered staff with staff, company with company, platoon with platoon. While respecting one another's need for time alone, we ate together, trained together, planned and conducted operations together. As the KNA grew more proficient, they assumed the lead in operations, and I often placed units under their operational control during missions.

I outlawed the use of the term "Jammers." I also demanded precision in referring to insurgents. I wanted to know if they were Takriri or Zari-Sattar or unaffiliated local militants. We needed to understand these distinctions and apply unique approaches in countering each of them.

Perhaps more importantly, I emphasized the importance of human contact and relationship building. I grew to learn from Naseem that relationships and perceptions are combat power. A worker at an outpost goes home every night and talks with his family and friends about how his day went and how he was treated. Word spreads quickly.

A shopkeeper at a bazaar discusses his business and, if we were in the area that day, whether we slimed his shop with dust or stopped by to talk and buy things. He would have every reason to support the planting of IEDs along the road if every time we passed by his shop we did damage to his livelihood. If we supported his livelihood, however, the calculus just might tip in our favor.

"They will respect you as a soldier," Naseem said one evening, "once they respect you as a man."

Testing a New Approach in Nargul

Naseem and I met with Bar Pak and Al'a Dust repeatedly. We questioned Bar Pak about the main priorities of the people in the province and in key areas such as Nargul and Mirgul. He gave very general answers— they wanted jobs and money and development and security. It became pretty clear that he lacked the level of detail necessary to establish any meaningful priorities.

From Al'a Dust we learned about the very poor and rudimentary training of his police. Beforehand, we had ridiculed them as incompetents. Now we realized that we needed to build their proficiency. We developed a partnership model linking our companies with police companies and our platoons with police stations. The partnership would be instrumental in building relationships, conducting "paramilitary" training, and holding them accountable.

Through the process of interacting at all levels, we formed an initial understanding of how communities governed themselves. Traditionally, the community councils consisted of elected leaders from the various tribes and clans. The number of seats on the council was based on proportion of the population. The council would elect a leader and a small senior council. The community councils would represent the people to the appointed government officials.

The council would operate on consensus. This was an honor-based society rather than a western legal-based society. The cultural and social norms of the communities meant that dishonor or disrespect demanded vengeance. Fairness was defined by proportional distribution of benefits and opportunities rather than by legal code. Unfairness toward a particular group was considered a corrupt practice. It meant disrespect, often threatened the livelihood of the excluded groups, and ultimately resulted in communal violence. Superempowerment of one group would result in the others creating alliances to attempt to rebalance the power.

Consensus ensured that all parties were fairly represented in every decision. This meant that decisions could take weeks or months—or longer. No decision was made unless consensus was assured beforehand. This was how they avoided exterminating themselves in blood feuds, and why the society was so conservative. I began to understand that most meetings were simply to talk, ventilate issues and perspectives, and lay out negotiating positions. Some of these meetings would erupt into heated arguments. Specially designated meetings were decision forums—formal ratification of consensus among all parties.

The council played a critical role in dispute resolution. They could put a dispute on ice until an appropriate resolution could be achieved. Sometimes that could take months, or even years. Once a matter was referred to or taken up by the council, the disputants were duty bound to cease recriminations until the council determined a solution and accountability.

In the small peaceful town of Shamgul, for instance, a man had returned home early from work and found his wife in bed with another man. He shot the man. The dead man's brother shot the brother of the shooter. Within four days, four more blood killings occurred. The council intervened to stop the killing from spreading. That was three years ago. The matter has not yet been resolved. Other disputes have lasted for decades.

Meeting the Nargul Council

Naseem and I asked Bar Pak to arrange a meeting with the Nargul area council so we could discuss critical needs and priorities.

Three days later, he brought the greater Nargul council to the governor's office for a meeting.

Bar Pak introduced Mo Dust as the council leader. Mo Dust introduced the twenty-member council.

Naseem and I introduced ourselves to each member and asked them about their tribe and clan. Mo Dust and Bar Pak both insisted that tribe and clan were no longer relevant. I told them that I had been studying the society and wanted to learn more.

Naseem had made a point earlier in the day that struck me. "Among the Torag tribe, we have a saying: 'God gave you two ears and two eyes but only one mouth.' The saying means that you should watch and listen twice as much as you speak."

I told him that we have a similar saying that one should seek to understand before trying to be understood. I had been walking around with my mouth open but my eyes and ears shut. That needed to change.

Within the twenty-member council, seventeen were from the Nar tribe and three were from the Mir. Only three of the four clans of the Nar were represented. All three Mir members were from the same clan.

"I really appreciate your meeting with me today," I began. "As you know, I am relatively new to your community and want to better understand your culture. I hope you can teach me."

The elders were nodding in agreement.

"I have heard a lot about councils and their importance. Can you please tell me what a council is and its importance in governing the community?"

Mo Dust stood and explained the basics of the council. It was the community's governing body. To keep all of the interests of the various groups fairly addressed, the council operated on full consensus. Sometimes decisions could take months or even years. The council was proportionally representative. The number of seats allocated was based on the percentage of the population of each tribe or clan in the community. Members were elected annually by their community. The council would then elect a leader and a small leadership group to assist him.

"So does the council leader make decisions for the community?" I asked.

"He is the spokesman for the council to the government," replied Mo Dust. He speaks for the consensus or lack of consensus of the group. He does not make decisions by himself. That is the council's job. He can call meetings, develop an agenda for discussion, and determine when to move to another subject."

"Okay, I think I understand." I rephrased what Mo Dust said in my own words just to make sure I had it right—and to show that I was genuinely listening and learning. The elders nodded as the interpreter put my words into their language.

"And how do the council and governor work together?"

Bar Pak explained that the council represented the people and the governor represented the government. Together they would make decisions. The council would resolve internal community disputes and make internal community decisions. The governor would deal with any disputes or problems the council put forward. He would work with the council to establish priorities and would request necessary support from the government on behalf of the people. He also reported the local situation to the central government.

I repeated what Bar Pak told me, and he and Mo Dust affirmed that I understood correctly. "I know there are many tribes and clans in Narabad. Can you tell me who they are?"

Most Dust reluctantly explained the four major tribes groups, the Nar, Mir, Zari, and Marzin. He also explained that the Nar, Mir, and Zari each had four clans, and the Marzin had two.

I repeated again what Mo Dust told me. "I'm puzzled," I said. "Why aren't any elders from the Zari or Marzin present? And what about the other clans of your tribes?"

"The Zari do not recognize the government," answered Bar Pak. "They believe they are part of Zaristan province rather than Narabad province." Zaristan was the province to the north and west.

"And the Marzin are criminals and land thieves! They are not real Khanastanis and do not belong on the council. They came here from Markhand many years ago and began taking our land and stealing our livestock." explained Mo Dust.

We had been getting a lot of violence from the north and west. "So who is responsible for the attacks north and west of here?" I anticipated the answer.

"The Zari rejectionists, supported by the criminal Marzin, are responsible for all of the violence there. They get support from Markhand. They follow a different religious school than the rest of us, which promotes violence." Mo Dust continued, "They need to be eliminated. Get rid of them and punish Markhand and you will solve all of the problems here."

"I think I understand. The Zari wish to be part of Zaristan. They do not accept being a part of Narabad and so refuse to join the council. They follow the Jamma Rhun rather than the Hambali school. The Marzin are not welcome because of their different ethnicity. And both groups are fighting. They seek assistance in their violence from Markhand."

Mo Dust confirmed that I understood the situation correctly. "Well, how about the Nar clan and three Mir clans that are not represented here?"

The elders began to look at one another as the words were translated and began conversing in a local dialect that the interpreter did not understand. This interpreter was good, but I needed to find someone as good who also understood this dialect.

"We have some of our own difficulties to address," Mo Dust said, as he looked at me and across the council. "But we want to talk with you about projects we need for our villages." He was clearly trying to change the subject.

"I understand that you wish to discuss development projects for your people." The elders nodded. "I have also learned from you about the importance of the council as representatives of all of the people in the area, and how the council and the government are supposed to work together. I also learned about the different tribes and clans in Narabad." After I listed them, Mo Dust looked at me approvingly.

"You learn very quickly, commander."

"You are very good teachers," I said. Teachers were valued members of the community, so I knew that would resonate. Naseem was clearly pleased at how I was handling the conversation.

"So how about projects?" Mo Dust inquired.

"Well, I think we should discuss that at another time. As you have taught me, the council represents the people, and I would not feel comfortable discussing projects unless the full council is together and all the clans and tribes have consensus on what they need for their communities. You have told me how delicate balancing all of these interests must be, so I would not want to put you in a position in which other tribes and clans felt you were cheating them, or that I was cheating them."

The elders again began talking in their local dialect, some of the conversation becoming a little heated. Mo Dust stopped the argument. I figured they did not want to argue in front of me. Even though I did not know what was being said, they knew that I would likely get the gist of the conversation from someone there.

"Very well, commander. We will organize the full council and then discuss projects."

We all shook hands in the way the Khan do—first placing the right hand over the other person's heart and then shaking hands. At first I thought they were trying to hug me, so I hugged them back. They thought that was kind of funny and they taught me their custom. We had a good laugh at my expense, but I think they appreciated that I could laugh at myself as well.

Bar Pak and Al'a Dust remained after the meeting.

"How did it go?" I asked.

"You did well," responded Bar Pak. "You showed them that you were willing to listen and learn. That was good. But I am very concerned that we will not get any projects in the area because the people have too much enmity. We should get projects going, then more people will come together."

Bar Pak may have had a point, but I also knew he had a personal agenda to enrich himself and his cronies from the projects.

After he departed, Al'a Dust pulled me and Naseem aside. "You did the right thing by showing that you listened and learned. People will respect that. You also did the right thing by requiring a proper council before making decisions that affect the community. Too many people are out for themselves here."

Making Connections

We continued to take enemy contact over the next several weeks. We conducted some significant combat operations to hit the insurgents when they were massing in the Zari and Mirgul areas, to deny them key terrain and keep them off balance. I had carefully emplaced a company near Mirgul, at the same spot from the last scenario, and positioned another one in the Zari area near the village of Nishigram. I kept an additional company at the main base in Nargul to conduct operations. I wanted to see how the situation developed before committing all or part of them to a fixed site.

Narabad was loosely organized into three general areas, although they were not formal government entities: Nargul, Mirgul, and Zari (the Marzin were present in each area as farmers and herders). The Nargul area council had still not come together. There was no council, at least not one that had met with us, for either the Mirgul or Zari areas. A proper Narabad council would not come about for a very long time.

The social fragmentation contributed to instability. As long as the fracturing continued, governance was impossible to organize effectively. Without organized governance and consensus, economic support or projects would not be effective—and could be counterproductive, as I had seen previously. Security would be hopeless—we could not kill our way out of a local insurgency, which, by definition, has public support or acquiescence.

The insurgents, especially the ideologically driven ones, I suspected, actively promoted the social fragmentation. It was certainly in their interests to do so. The more effectively they could undermine both official and traditional governance, the easier it would be for them to take control of communities.

Naseem and I began to develop some informal personal contacts to help us explore ideas in private. I needed to get a deeper understanding of society than was possible in a public forum. We tried to get a decent cross section of society—elders, younger men and women, and a few children. For the adults, my first sign of trustworthiness was whether they asked anything for themselves. I wanted people who did not. More often than not, I found, the most trustworthy ones desperately desired education for their children. They had seen the effects on their communities as education was undermined during the decades of violence. A return to social normalcy and community health required educated young men and women, not illiterate fighters.

I learned pretty quickly that in the traditional order, elders, religious leaders, and teachers formed the social nexus of community governance. These traditional authority figures represented a combination of recognized social status (landholding elites), religious authority, and leadership ability recognized through education, problem-solving, and social skills. Teachers were highly celebrated in the society. They represented the long-term viability and prosperity of the community.

The Situation in Zari—
Things are Not Always as They Seem

During one of my many personal conversations, I asked about a certain Zari insurgent leader named Sher Wali. My interlocutor, Afzal, was from the Nar tribe, but he lived in Popgul, which was fairly close to the Zari area. He knew the society there very well.

"What would you like to know about him?"

"Well, first of all, why is he so powerful?"

Afzal knotted his brows and said, "He is not very powerful at all."

"Please explain." I was struck by Afzal's comment. Sher Wali could bring roughly fifty to a hundred well-trained and well-armed fighters to a fight. "He seems to command a lot of fighters."

"That he does. But he does not have a big house or any land. He does not have any sons, and his two daughters are young. He is clever but not educated, and he is not from the first family of the tribe. He does have access to money and guns; he has shown himself to be a good military leader, but that is all he knows."

Fascinating. What Afzal just described to me as "power" was defined in traditional terms. One with a big house and a lot of land and livestock could help provide for the community. Having a lot of sons, or daughters who could marry into big families, would create social connectivity that could be influential in a council or a dispute. Being educated would help to bring prosperity to the community and to educate the next generation.

Sher Wali was none of those. He had street cred as a relatively poor man who had risen through the ranks to a leadership position in the Zari-Sattar during the many years of fighting. He had access to money and guns. He represented political, social, and economic opportunity to other poor men in the community. With little education or economic potential in the area, many poor men had a choice between being subsistence farmers for life or having the opportunity to make money and gain status through fighting. As the persistent fighting in the area indicated, many were taking the latter option.

Sher Wali, of course, was perfectly happy to undermine the traditional order. A return to social normalcy could be a threat to his personal power. After the Markhand wars, most of the elders, preachers, and teachers had gone back to their homes and families, expecting "normal" life to continue. Sher Wali and others had different ideas. They went into smuggling timber and gems and other materials—black-market, criminal enterprises that leveraged the old logistical routes and required "security forces" to protect the business. The Khanastan government's attempt to regulate timber and gem trade by essentially outlawing it through punitive taxes and painful bureaucracy played into the hands of the smuggling networks.

In essence, Sher Wali represented a new and rising form of power—one based on money, guns, and illegal smuggling. He gained control of the youth and used them as coercive instruments. He began enforcing Domol-style social norms on the people.

When the new Khanastan government came to power, supported with forces from the international community, Sher Wali and others simply expanded their operations to include insurgency—aided and abetted by elements within Markhand.

What the more traditional figures failed to realize, as so often happens, was that this rising new power was in direct competition with them for authority. The traditional figures assumed they could control people like Sher Wali—that society would simply return to normal with them in charge. However, Sher Wali, like so many others, slowly gained the upper hand. As these traditional figures clung to an old paradigm, they grew increasingly irrelevant and unable to govern.

"I had not thought about society in this way," Naseem told me privately when I told him about my insight. "I think your conclusions are very sound."

In many ways, the main conflict was the competition for political power and social control between the traditional "tribal aristocracy" and the rising militant class. And the traditional figures did not even realize it—nor would they until it was too late.

I directed my intelligence staff to examine this further. Sure enough, the majority of insurgent leaders in the area had backgrounds similar to Sher Wali's. Bala Khan, an exception, was from the traditional order.

The same phenomenon was happening, in a more advanced stage, across the border in Markhand. Elders and educators were increasingly marginalized. Eventually, they were given the choice to cooperate, leave, or be killed. A recent series of murders of scores of elders in Markhand was an object lesson. If the same process got too far in Narabad, the situation could become irreversible.

Respect for tradition within communities was one important social factor that offered potential. We needed to determine how to subtly reinforce peaceful, traditional mechanisms and social normalcy without undermining them in the process.

This problem in many areas centered on the lack of governance and social cohesion—without functioning councils and credible governance mechanisms, we were not going to arrest or reverse the social momentum of leaders like Sher Wali.

But Bala Khan was an influential leader from the traditional order, so it was unlikely that he would feel the need to overthrow it. Perhaps Mirgul had a functioning council and we just did not know it. If so, the council was probably responding to the desires of the people.

The many insurgencies in Narabad were self-organizing social movements. They needed only sufficient "agency" to materialize. That agency came in the forms of militant leaders like Sher Wali or community leaders like Bala Khan. They highlighted issues such as official abuse of power and social exclusion by the government, civilian casualties and other practices by international forces that angered the population, lack of social and economic opportunity within communities, and local community conflict, and used them to gain support. These problems created demand-signals for insurgency.

The senior insurgent leaders saw the real fight in terms of community control.

They employed a social strategy of gaining a foothold in communities, exploiting grievances and problems to build up militant cells—ostensibly to "protect" the community. The armed and funded cells would gradually gain control of the community. The senior leaders would link controlled communities together through militant networks, expanding the areas under their control from the bottom up.

Fighting against us and the government forces was a means to the real end: political and social control. Fighting was used to demonstrate credibility and create more reasons for fighting and thus greater need for protection by the local militants. It was an innovative, almost brilliant, bottom-up strategy.

We needed to provide subtle agency to an alternative self-organizing social movement while reducing the other factors that promoted insurgency. We needed to beat the insurgents' bottom-up strategy by promoting an alternative bottom-up strategy, complemented by demonstrating that the future of the communities was better assured by peaceful, representative, local councils working together with an increasingly credible government, all of which were supported by us until they could stand on their own.

Of course, there were limits to how much we could make this all happen. We could provide a spark and organize incentives, but the communities would need to take ownership and act of their own volition.

One advantage that we had was the ability to meet the positive needs and desires of communities. The insurgents offered a political voice and economic opportunity, but those "benefits" centered on violence, which ultimately offered nothing to the community.

I finally understood what Alex had meant by the people and communities being the most important actors in the environment. To defeat a local insurgency, social intolerance and active measures against insurgent activity were necessary. We needed to help facilitate that in order to defeat the insurgent groups.

Adapting to the Environment—
Creating and Using Leverage

Alex had once mentioned a Chinese game called Go. Insurgency and counterinsurgency more closely resembled Go than they did chess. Unlike chess, Go starts with a blank board. Each side takes turns placing stones on the board. Contiguous stones represent territorial control as the board gets filled over time. The object of the game is to win more control of territory than your opponent. Therefore, you want to create your own secure spaces and connect them into contiguous areas while breaking apart those of your adversary.

The analogy is not perfect, of course. In counterinsurgency, you do not begin with a blank slate, and in some cases, the insurgency already has a huge advantage in popular support or control. And as in the multi-dimensional chess game discussed earlier, there are more than two players.

Nonetheless, we would need to create a strategy similar to one successful in Go—create friendly contiguous areas hardened against penetration while disrupting and breaking apart the areas under enemy control. Make the enemy focus on competing for increasingly smaller and more isolated areas. That is how we would gain and maintain the initiative.

We would need to start in places that had sufficient social cohesion and, ideally, connections with other communities. Hardening these communities against insurgent penetration and facilitating their connection would begin to create contiguous friendly areas. Social relationships from these areas would give us a foothold into contested ones. Over time, we would need to penetrate, contest, and defeat the insurgency in those areas, too.

I directed my intelligence staff to work together with Naseem's staff to prepare a map that overlaid social cohesion and social connections with geography and insurgent activity so we could better appreciate where the opportunities and challenges existed. This took a lot of investigation and conversation during patrols, engagement with key leaders, and interaction at all levels on the streets and in villages.

Our junior leaders developed all sorts of innovative techniques to derive this information, from games and sports to marking certain goods and watching their flow through different communities. Biometric data was also useful in seeing how the population moved. The picture of social relationships and connectivity gave us a more sophisticated understanding of the environment and key communities to contest.

Our company commanders and platoon leaders had been meeting with local village and community councils, emphasizing that a properly and proportionally representative council was necessary before discussing substantive issues beyond information gathering and relationship building. We knew that the representativeness would grow over time, and the real community leaders would emerge and participate as the process gained credibility.

We learned from Naseem that the influential elders in contested areas would not be the first ones to meet with us. Because they were uncertain of our intentions, they did not want to risk putting their honor on the line if we turned out to be threats to their society. So they usually sent "front men" to see what the foreigners or outsiders were up to. If the front men determined that our intentions were good and we were not a threat, and if they believed we could benefit the community, then the elders would agree to meet with us. In other words, we had to pass a test.

But these front men would not be the only ones we would see initially. Opportunists would seek us out, offering support and information in the hope of gaining money, power, and influence. The opportunists were out for themselves; they were seen as threats to the social order. If we superempowered them, the population was likely to turn against us.

We had to be careful. Working with the councils as a collective body would help us avoid that pitfall . . . and help us avoid unintentionally fostering social friction.

Once we had momentum at local levels, we wanted to build toward larger-area councils and eventually one for the province.

At Naseem's suggestion, we employed a deliberate confidence-building process with the community councils, beginning with smaller issues and eventually working toward larger and more delicate ones. The first step consisted of meetings and relationship building. Willingness to meet with us and government officials routinely was an important signal of social cohesion and willingness to work together.

The meetings also served as a barometer of insurgent control. The communities under insurgent influence would find reasons to not meet with us. Those under the control of the council would meet on a regular schedule. Sometimes meeting with us and other times not became an indicator of a contested area.

The second step involved coordination of simple issues such as humanitarian assistance, delivery of school supplies, and developing a prioritized list of community needs. This step provided us an opportunity to show that we respected community governance and that we were willing to work together with the councils on behalf of the people. Once a relationship was built, we needed to move quickly into testing mutual credibility.

We wanted to see if the councils could meet simple governance deliverables. For instance, they would be required to organize a humanitarian assistance delivery event in their community. Once we agreed to conduct the event, the council would be required at the next meeting to give a list of the names of people in need of humanitarian assistance and the nature of those needs. At the next meeting, we would have the goods on hand, and the council, police, army, government officials, and we would organize the goods into packages for specific people. We would then agree upon a date for delivery in the village.

My soldiers, KNA, and the police would get the supplies to the village, but the elders ran the event itself, together with a government official. KNA and police and my soldiers would provide security in coordination with the council. This enabled us to visit the village at the invitation of the council and to meet people and gather more information. The council showed credibility that they could work together with us on behalf of the community.

Humanitarian assistance events were not primarily designed to win "hearts and minds" but to strengthen our relationship, promote local governance, and set conditions for affecting the cost-benefit equation in communities. We wanted the council to get the "win" for the event, but we also wanted to meet people on their own turf and show them that we could be partners with the community and not simply aliens from a different country that brought nothing but violence.

Once this step was met satisfactorily—we normally did a few iterations—we moved on to small-scale economic support. Once again, the burden fell primarily on the councils. They needed to develop a list of priorities for the community and present it at a meeting. They would then invite us to the village to show us where they intended the project to be built. These events included tea with the council, at a minimum, and sometimes a larger feast.

In the culture of Khanastan, the invitation meant the council guaranteed our safety in the village. We would often request the council meet us at an outpost or agreed location and walk or drive with us to the village. This served as an additional message to the people that the council requested our presence and also served a deterrent effect from an insurgent attack en route to or returning from the village.

We wanted to put the insurgents in lose-lose dilemmas. If they failed to fight, they lost credibility. If they attacked a patrol escorted by the elders, they turned the people against them. Our aggressive overwatch also guaranteed the militants would pay a heavy price for an attack. If they allowed a project to occur in their village, the council was strengthened in the eyes of the people, and potential fighters got jobs. If the militants attacked a project owned by the village, the people would turn against them.

Of course, the insurgents would adapt to this approach. The most skillful insurgents combine coercion and attraction quite artfully to control the population, and they will not give up such control easily. We would need to anticipate and sense changes in the environment and make our counteradaptations.

The invitation to the village also served as an indicator of control. Naturally, we would not get invited to an insurgent-controlled village that was ideologically opposed to our presence. We might get invited to a contested village if the insurgents had an open mind. Generally, an invitation meant the council was in charge—at least at that point in time.

The visit allowed us to confirm that the places they intended for the projects were largely appropriate. They also provided another opportunity to be present in a village and talk with people in a positive venue.

Once that test was met satisfactorily, we would require the council to draw up project proposals for their top-priority projects. If they lacked the expertise, then they would have to hire an engineer to develop the proposal. This was another significant departure from previous practice in which we or outside engineers would do it for them.

The proposal needed to include the technical specifications of the job as well as identification of the management and accountant, the amount and cost of labor and materials, and resolution of land donation.

We wanted to make the process as labor-intensive as possible. The village needed to show that they wanted the project badly enough to go through the trouble. If they sweated for it, they would protect it.

Once the proposal was satisfactory, we would arrange for approval and obtain the initial payment. Naseem advised that if the area had local insurgent activity, we should inform the council and the people that we could not in good conscience give the initial payment until the security situation changed because of the risk the money would get stolen or the project destroyed.

The council had to make a choice whether they wanted to deliver for their own people or to let local insurgents run amok. This was another way we learned to create leverage. The members of the council were elected to bring benefits to the village. If they failed to deliver for the village, chances were pretty good that they would not get elected the next time. Their honor in the eyes of their villagers was on the line. More often than not, they reined in local thugs so they could make good on their promise to the people. We used a carrot as a stick—another way to affect the cost-benefit equation.

If the situation was satisfactory, then we would deliver the initial payment. Subsequent payments required more visits to the village to verify the progress of the work and check the accounting. The full details of the project had to be made available to all villagers. Our visits would enable us to check that. The transparency reinforced accountability and served to mitigate concerns over corruption.

We found that projects done by this method were completed more quickly and to a higher standard—and with far fewer security problems—than those built by outsiders. The honor of the council was on the line for the project to be completed correctly. They had complete ownership; the project success was solely their responsibility. Failure meant being undermined in the eyes of the people, and the likelihood that they would not prevail in the next council elections.

This approach used projects as a tool to build and strengthen governance. Governance that was responsive to the needs of the people was rewarded with popular support. And communities with strong governance were generally hardened against militant penetration.

Our confidence-building approach grew more sophisticated over time. Each meeting would end with a review of the commitments each party had made to one another for delivery, and an agreement on two to three open issues that would be discussed at the next meeting—which had a set date and time. The subsequent meeting began with a review of the deliverables and the previously agreed-to agenda items. If one side failed to make the deliverable, then progress on the issue stopped, the problems were discussed, and a plan of action was developed.

This process allowed us to accomplish several objectives. First, we got a good sense of who was in charge of the community. Second, we were developing and exercising local governance. Third, we were building mutual trust and credibility in one another and in each of us in the eyes of the community. Fourth, we were building a mechanism for checks and balances between the community, the council that represented it, and government officials who were always present during the process.

The process also gave tangible expression of the benefits of the village, government, and us working together. By creating the potential for economic opportunity and improvements in the quality of living in the community, we also developed a meaningful way of imposing costs for lack of performance or tolerance for insurgent activity.

The process was not always smooth—we had plenty of bumps along the way that required us to adapt. In the village of Kamgul, for instance, something quite unexpected occurred.

Kamgul was located in a capillary valley southeast of Nargul, populated by Nar and some Mir and Marzin. It had some previous insurgent activity, but gradually became a relatively peaceful village located in an area we wanted to influence. As the confidence-building process developed, and governance and economic support got under way, a contest for council membership emerged in the village.

A group of obviously poor, younger men arrived at the outpost requesting to see my company commander and the KNA commander responsible for the area. They introduced themselves as the "new council" for Kamgul. My company commander and his KNA counterpart met with them and heard their story. While they were meeting, the "old council" from Kamgul arrived—an older and relatively more well-to-do group.

Being quick on his feet, my company commander informed each group individually that he would always be happy to speak with any individual or group that wanted to talk, but that he would only do business with one council from the village. Once they worked out the composition of the council and introduced themselves to the governor, police, KNA commander, and himself, then business could resume.

Later we understood what had happened. The "old council" represented all of the tribes and clans, but a number of have-nots within the village had abstained from voting for the council. As the council's credibility grew, the have-nots—who were likely previous supporters of insurgent activity—decided that they now wanted to be involved and formed their own council. After about a month of deliberations, the village elected a new council that wound up including members of both groups.

As mutual trust and credibility grew with the village councils, we found that the representativeness of the group expanded, and that the more influential elders began becoming active members. The key influencers would generally hold back until the process demonstrated sufficient credibility in their eyes. They were not willing to put their honor on the line to participate in something unproven.

The process radically expanded our understanding of the political and social dynamics of the area. Credible relationships enabled us to begin discussing more delicate security issues—we developed a much greater understanding of the insurgency as well.

As the council's credibility increased, we could move on to a final stage of confidence building that involved joint efforts to deal with security issues. If we or the army or the police received a report of a weapons cache in or near a village, we would discuss the matter and request that the council escort us to the location. The search would be conducted by the council and the army and police together, which reinforced governance and prevented any pilfering from the home. The police gained respectability in the process as well.

Finally, we would establish a written agreement that would codify how the government, the council, the army, the police, and we foreign troops would work together.

Over time, our influence expanded in the Nargul area to the point at which a properly representative area council emerged that we could work with on larger issues.

And we began creating footholds in the more difficult Mirgul area.

We used a different approach to gain the views of women. Instead of forcing a percentage of women on a town council, we formed "female engagement teams" like those the Marines used in Afghanistan. These teams of women would go on patrols and interact with women in villages and bazaars. They would also hold meetings in villages with groups of women. Over time, some villages allowed the women's groups to meet on an outpost. Our knowledge of the local environment grew substantially.

And we soon found out that women were quite influential, albeit behind the scenes. Once a women's group agreed to something, it was not long before the village council was raising the same issue.

Recognizing the scarcity of women's health care in the area, I asked the brigade for female medics and doctors. My partner battalions readily gave them up, so I was able to deploy female medics to all the major outposts and had a female doctor rotate time at each one. We soon had significant numbers of women going to the aid station for treatment. Our medics, after coordination with the elders, also trained selected women in basic first aid and some more advanced skills so they could serve their communities.

The increase in support from the women was often a leading indicator of increased support from the village population.

There was still plenty of fighting in Narabad, and we conducted operations in the countryside to disrupt insurgent groups or serve as a deterrent. We certainly affected the supply-side of the equation. But we did not let those operations take on lives of their own and distract us from focus on the demand side. We needed to dislocate the insurgents from the sources of their strength.

As Alex pointed out one day, a real offensive operation takes from the enemy what he cannot afford to lose. In a counterinsurgency, especially one with local support, the enemy can afford to lose fighters and weapons—there were many more to be had. What he could not afford to lose was the support or acquiescence of the population. That is what we aimed to take away.

Initial Progress in Zari

Nonetheless, we were having little luck, and a lot of contact, in the more remote Zari tribal area, except for the village of Nishigram, which was near one of our outposts. We began sending messages with people who had relatives in the area and also broadcast on the radio and local newspaper our request to meet with Zari village councils. We particularly wanted to meet with elders from the main Zari village of Zargram, which was about fifteen kilometers along a mountain river valley from Nishigram. This effort went on for a couple months.

One day, a group of very poor men arrived at the Nishigram outpost. They announced themselves as the Zargram council and said they were responding to a request for a meeting. My company commander and his KNA counterpart at the outpost agreed to meet with them. He began by asking what tribe they were from. They all responded that they were Marzin.

My company commander and the KNA commander discussed with them why we were in the area, that we wanted to build a relationship with the Zari people and determine ways we could work together.

We implemented another of Naseem's suggestions. We developed a set of "listening points" (rather than only "talking points") for each meeting—these were key issues we wanted to learn about from the meeting so we could better understand the environment. My company commander had elicited one key point already—these men were Marzin not Zari. Their body language indicated that they were frightened. He figured that these were "scouts" from the Zari elders, who were sending their farmers to see what we really wanted.

He knew that he had to reassure them of their safety and our good intentions. He listened carefully to everything they had to say, had one of his troopers take notes, and repeated back to them the key points they had made. As the meeting concluded, he gave them some food for their journey and trouble and asked them to return in two weeks after speaking with their community about their priorities.

Naseem and I were visiting the Nishigram outpost two weeks later when another group arrived and announced that they were the Zargram council and were responding to our request to talk. Naseem and I and our company commanders met with them. I asked what tribe they were from. They were also Marzin.

The men were clearly frightened—even more so because Naseem and I were there. These were some of the poorest men I had ever seen. Their main spokesman shook with anxiety as he talked. Another man was clumsily drinking water—it was the first time in his life he had taken water from a bottle.

The men spoke in the local dialect to one another, so I also brought an interpreter who understood the Marzin dialect. I wanted him to listen for any side conversations.

We discussed the usual subjects—our desire to work together with the council and the people, gain feedback on their concerns and needs, and understand their perspective. Naseem and I used a good deal of active listening to make sure we understood their points, and to ensure they knew we understood them.

Afterwards, I asked them if they had seen our aid station. Of course, they had not. I took them to our doctors at the outpost and explained that we could help if anyone from their village or tribe got sick until the government or a business could set up a clinic. I asked if they had any ailments. Each of them did. The docs took good care of them. We then parted ways, asking them to return in a week or so with a list of priorities.

The side conversations our interpreter overheard were interesting. The men remarked how well our soldiers treated them, that we apparently did not intend on killing them or putting them in jail, and how genuinely we seemed to want to work together. Exactly the outcome I wanted.

Ten days later, another group of Marzin men arrived at the outpost to meet with the company commanders. The same outcome occurred as after the other two meetings.

A week after that, something interesting happened. A group of well-dressed men arrived at the Nishigram outpost, requesting to see the company commanders. They introduced themselves as the council from Zargram. The KNA company commander asked what tribe they were from. "Zari," they responded. Now we had real elders from the town.

The meeting format and content was the same as previous ones: key listening points about their perspectives and priorities, paying attention to verbal or body language cues that indicated an issue of particular interest or anxiety. The elders focused on the violence and fear and lack of support.

My company commander asked them whether they supported the government or the insurgents.

Their answer was revealing: "We are on nobody's side in this war, because no one is on our side. The government robs us, the foreign forces bomb us, and the militants beat us. This is not our war, but we are caught in the middle of it. We want to be free from violence, free to live our own lives, and free to build a future for our children—education, jobs, good health."

With their strong history of independence, the Zari were unlikely to choose a side, so to speak, but we might be able to determine enough objectives in common that we could help one another achieve them.

As the meeting concluded, the elders started laughing after exchanging some comments in the Zari dialect. My commander asked them what was the matter.

"The militants said that the only reason you wanted us to come here was so you could kill us or put us in jail. We believed them for months. As you might have guessed, we sent three parties of our farmers to see what you really wanted. When they all came back with the same story about your sincerity and kindness, we decided to see for ourselves. We can't believe we were foolish enough to listen to the militants."

They all got a good chuckle from the story. We now had a foothold in the important Zargram village and would use the confidence-building process to strengthen the relationship and undermine the militants.

The Enemy Adapts— Hitting the Wall in Mirgul and Zari

The Mir area was more difficult to crack. Part of the reason was that Bala Khan was genuinely influential beyond the money and guns and had the active support of the people.

He had been wronged by Bar Pak and had a long-standing feud with Al'a Dust from the Markhand wars, based on some incident between their two forces. Bar Pak saw him as a rival influence and no doubt had reported him as an insurgent leader to our special forces a year or so ago. Bala Khan was opposed to foreign presence in the area, perhaps due to his experiences in the Markhand war and the fact that he had been the target of a U.S. raid in the past. His relatives across the border provided a base of support and supplies.

We got a little traction in a handful of Mir villages, but not enough to make any significant difference in the levels of violence or militant control.

I was experiencing similar roadblocks elsewhere. A few Nar villages remained in enemy hands and much of the Zari area was under insurgent control as well.

I was missing something in the cost-benefit equation in the areas under stronger insurgent control. We hit those areas repeatedly with our own and special forces–enabled raids, but we never quite had enough to target the main insurgent leaders, such as Sher Wali and Bala Khan and others. The militants kept regenerating. The councils never materialized in those areas.

We had reduced the areas of insurgent control and had moved many contested villages to our side. But now our approach was running into a surface that we could not seem to penetrate.

The enemy, moreover, began to adapt.

Night letters and intimidation campaigns began targeting the council members in the more contested villages.

In the Zari areas, for instance, our efforts began to take hold in Zargram and some surrounding villages, but we could get no real traction in the more inaccessible valleys. Some of the village councils that had held initial meetings with us gradually stopped coming. Some elders had family members kidnapped, others had their houses burned; some had been shot at and a few killed.

I asked one of the chief Zargram elders, Ar Rahim, for his advice.

"These people need protection. They are interested in working together but are not yet strong enough to do so. We need a tribal police."

I replied that the KNA commander, police chief, and I could give him fifty police and soldiers for protection. But Ar Rahim replied, "We cannot accept the government police for our villages. Besides, there are not enough of them." I understood the point about wanting protection but could not figure out why he would not accept police.

"You also need to know that some of these people who are fighting are not bad people," Ar Rahim added. "They have their reasons for fighting that need to be addressed. You need to offer them an alternative and peace."

I said that I would be happy to grant them peace if the militants surrendered and the leaders turned themselves over to the police.

"You must understand something about our people. They will not surrender. Most will negotiate to end a conflict, but they do not give up. And when they feel they are weak, they will simply fight back harder and to the death."

I objected that we did not negotiate with terrorists. The militants were relatives and kinsmen of the elders. If they surrendered, we would treat them well. Why couldn't Ar Rahim and the elders persuade them to give up?

"We are not strong enough on our own to do that—and their grievances are not with us. Their problems are with the government and the foreigners. You are the stronger party; you have to make the first move. If you do not, then you will have two Zaris—one neutral and one firmly in the hands of the militants."

"Then so be it."

"Then we will be doomed to perpetual fighting as long as you are here. You have proven yourself to be a man of war, and we think you care for the people. But that is not enough to bring peace. People have to believe there is an end to the violence, that peace is an option. Then they will take risk for it."

"And there will be peace once these people stop fighting."

After the conversation, Naseem asked me to consider their request. He thought their points were valid. The women's groups were especially forward-leaning on peace with the nonideological insurgents. I told him that we had to draw the line somewhere. I was not going to negotiate with terrorists.

"Not all who are fighting are terrorists," replied Naseem. "Some you must fight; some you can overcome without fighting. Wisdom is in knowing the difference. You will be respected as a man of war if you are first seen as a man of peace."

"But these people are shooting at us!"

"You seem to believe that it is right and just for you to shoot at them but not for them to shoot at you. This thinking is strange to me. I think it clouds your judgment. Is it not possible that people on both sides see their own cause as just?"

Initial Debrief

Alex stopped the simulation here and came down to meet me and Mick in the debriefing area. This was by far the longest scenario yet, lasting well into the evening. I was exhausted.

"This was an interesting scenario. What is your assessment and where do we go from here?"

I told Alex that I thought I was finally starting to get it. We had far better results this time than any other. Levels of violence had dropped substantially, and areas under insurgent control had contracted. We had solidified our hold in most of the Nar area and had a functioning council that had begun tackling larger problems. We had made inroads on the Zari area, particularly in the main town of Zargram. We'd had a little traction in the Mir areas.

I was concerned, however, that our success was leveling off. We could not penetrate most of the areas that were under insurgent control, and in the more contested villages, the enemy had seemed to adapt and use intimidation tactics to keep the village away from our influence.

"It is hard to get people to take huge personal risks," said Alex validating my concern.

"Then you'll just have to hit them harder," Mick interrupted. "Look, I was really skeptical about this approach you were taking, and I'm still not fully convinced it will work in real life—but I have to admit that I learned something. But now you're going to have to knock some heads much harder. You know the villages and areas under insurgent control. Hit them—hard!" He pounded the table for added emphasis.

"That's an approach worth considering," Alex said. "What other options do you have?"

"I could sustain the status quo, continue to harden the friendly areas, work on the contested villages, and keep contracting insurgent influence. I'm concerned that we don't have the forces to protect the population in so many contested and enemy-controlled areas. I could redeploy some forces to those places, but not enough to really make a difference."

"Let's talk about Ar Rahim's advice," Alex suggested.

"He wanted me to give him tribal police—essentially to arm the population—and make peace with the insurgents. But I'm leery of the risks associated with arming the people or permitting them to openly arm themselves. And I am not going to negotiate with terrorists."

"Naseem made an interesting point," observed Alex. "Are they all terrorists?"

"Well, they have killed and wounded my soldiers. That makes them evil actors in my book."

"Is killing unusual in war?" asked Alex.

"Not at all. But we are here to help the people and the government. The insurgents are here to harm the people and kill my soldiers. The violence is their fault. If they stop fighting and pack it in, then the violence will stop."

Alex pressed the issue further. "Do they believe that they have legitimate reasons to fight?"

"Maybe they made themselves believe that they do."

"Let's talk about a few examples. What are Bala Khan's reasons for fighting?"

"Come on, Alex, are you some sort of apologist for insurgents?" Mick asked in frustration. "These people are evil. They killed Americans—his Americans. They need to be killed or captured. They can dream up all the excuses they wish. At the end of the day, they are bad people who do bad things and need to be taken off the battlefield permanently. Period."

I had to side with Mick on this one. I had given them the option to turn themselves in and they would be treated well. They chose not to take it. The fight goes on.

"Humor me, then," Alex insisted. "Why is Bala Khan fighting?"

"He has a problem with Bar Pak and Al'a Dust. He hates foreigners from his Markhand experience and the ways they treated the population in the past. The coalition organized raids to kill or capture him; there have been some civilian casualties among his relatives. He knows he is on our target list. He is a timber smuggler and power broker who has a large, publicly supported, organized crime gang."

"So he has an active feud ongoing with the governor and police chief," Alex summarized. "He has seen foreigners abuse the population and members of his family in the past. Our forces have targeted him. What happened to his timber mill?"

"The timber mill outside of Mirgul was bombed in one of the special forces' raids prior to our arrival. Bala Khan was reported to be in there. He owned the mill."

"So the governor and police chief are using the power of the state to pursue him as a personal enemy. We are helping them with that. We destroyed his business, which has forced him into smuggling. And he and his family suffered atrocities from the Markand war. His past experiences with foreigners have not been good ones."

"But we are not the Markhand army. We're the good guys."

"Maybe Bala Khan feels the same way—that he is the good guy," suggested Alex. "Put yourself in his shoes for a moment. Not to excuse him, but to see things from his perspective. That's part of knowing the enemy and knowing the environment."

I had a hard time wrapping my mind around that. I could accept that Bala Khan might believe he had legitimate reasons to fight. But he had still killed some of my soldiers, and I was not willing to get past that.

Mick summarized what I was feeling. "Regardless of whether he thinks he is fighting for a good reason or not, the fact of the matter is that he is an insurgent and an evil actor. He killed our soldiers. He needs to go."

"Perhaps so," said Alex. "What about Sher Wali?"

"Sher Wali is a hard-line religious and political ideologue. He is fighting to take control of the Zari area and impose his zealotry on the population. His main power center in Pitigram is his perverted dystopia."

"Do you see a difference between the motives of the two men?" Alex asked.

"One believes he has a legitimate cause for fighting back. The other simply wants power. Bala Khan's issues may have the potential for a resolution. Sher Wali's don't."

"But both of them have killed Americans, so they both need to pay for it," interjected Mick.

"You are going to have to determine," said Alex, "whether you want vengeance or whether you want to win. Sometimes you cannot have both."

Feedback Session

The techs had arrived with the tape. The readout matched my understanding of what had happened fairly well. The part that interested me was what was happening in the more contested villages.

Your outreach into contested villages stirred up significant discussions among the people. Some sided with talking and engagement, while others argued that they could not trust the Americans and the government. The areas contested by Sher Wali experienced the highest and most violent forms of intimidation—murder, rape, kidnapping. The elders were unable to protect themselves and their families. People began to blame them for bringing violence to the villages. The elders decided to stop meeting with you.

Those areas contested by Bala Khan experienced far less violent intimidation. The arguments there focused on whether the government and the Americans were sincere. Bala Khan and his supporters maintained that this was a trick to lure him and others into the open. When the Americans were asked whether they were willing to talk, they replied that they do not negotiate with terrorists. That was proof enough for people that the Americans and the government were not sincere. After that determination was made, the elders from various contested villages stopped meeting with you.

The hour was getting very late. I needed to think through this issue—both on an operational and a moral plane. Dispassionately, I could see Alex's point. Maybe Bala Khan and others had "legitimate" reasons to fight, from their perspective. But they had killed some of my soldiers and wounded others. That was unacceptable. Would making some sort of peace with him be a betrayal of my wounded and dead? But did I want others to get killed or wounded in continued fighting over problems that seemed to have possible solutions?

Sher Wali was beyond the pale—that decision was easy. But maybe Bala Khan was not irreconcilable. That moral dilemma kept me awake all night. This was not something the schoolhouse prepared us to consider.

If it was this hard to think through in simulation, how much more difficult would it be when real soldiers with real families got killed or wounded? What would I tell the soldier's widow or parents or children? "We made peace with the man responsible for your son's death?" Or would I be more content explaining to families, "I rejected a way to make peace because this insurgent had killed others, and as a result your son or husband or father was killed"? Or would I just live with guilt either way and keep it all to myself?

Why was I only now, after twenty years in service, thinking through this for the first time?

Mick was not troubled by such issues. For him, this was simple good and evil, and that mentality made him relentless. But Mick, as I was growing to learn, was a terrible counterinsurgent. He was great in a firefight, but how many of these firefights were really necessary? How many soldiers had lost their lives and limbs because of this overly simplistic outlook? How many areas had he stabilized? None, if I recalled. In fact, violence got worse every time. The explanation was that he always had the toughest areas. Was that really true?

Under what conditions is making peace the right decision . . . or the wrong decision? We could maybe make peace with Sher Wali and cede him control of Pitigram and surrounding areas, but the atrocities he and his henchmen inflicted upon the population and his abuse of women's and human rights were abhorrent. Were those really redlines? Would I be prepared to have my soldiers bleed and die to uphold them? Was there any way to guarantee that Sher Wali would remain content? Or would he use the respite to prepare to expand the areas under his control? These discussions and decisions might be easy in the halls of power away from the fight and the human consequences. It was different here.

As I thought more about the issues, Naseem's advice once again seemed correct. There was a difference between those fighting for practical reasons and those bent on personal power and imposition of an extreme ideology that would undermine our interests.

My Key Lessons

Work with communities for common objectives. They might not take your side, but you can make an alliance of convenience that enables you to work together for mutual benefit. Getting them to side with stability and community prosperity will increase their intolerance for insurgent violence.

Find creative ways to engage women. Even in highly patriarchal societies, women can be quite influential behind the scenes. Forcing gender integration on governance structures in such societies can be counterproductive and actually set back the goal of inclusion. But when engaged creatively, women will offer insights that men are either unwilling to discuss or don't see at all.

Create common understanding. Develop a shared, adaptive mental model that helps to explain the nature of the conflict and your game plan for success. The mental model should include issues such as whether the insurgency is local or nonlocal or a combination, the key drivers of instability, core interests of key actors (insurgents, government, local leaders), and your broad game plan for how to defeat the insurgency and develop resilient local stability. Communicate it relentlessly—the mental model must be *internalized* by every member of the unit. Encourage your team at all levels to challenge and adjust the mental model, especially as key actors adapt. The model will never be perfect, and you will need to refine it as you learn and adapt. Do not fall in love with the model—be ready to throw it out entirely and develop a new one if necessary.

Distinguish between the reconcilable and irreconcilable. Some insurgents are fighting for what they believe are entirely legitimate, practical reasons. Others fight for personal power and ideology. Force them to reveal their true colors. Co-opt the reconcilable; kill, capture, eliminate the irreconcilable.

The reconcilables need an alternative to fighting. Offering a way out to insurgents is a way to take the moral high ground in the eyes of communities. The people do not want violence in their areas, but they also do not want to see their relatives harmed—especially if they perceive the local insurgents to be fighting for legitimate reasons. Your efforts are likely to level out if you do not create an honorable way out of a cycle of violence.

Understand the human terrain in terms of relationships. Many of those will be familial, but some are business and other common interests. Knowing who connects to whom and over what interests gives you an ability to influence key people indirectly and eventually bring the reconcilable ones to work for common objectives.

Peace may not require capitulation. Those fighting due to legitimate grievances, particularly in an honor-based society, are very unlikely to accept an outcome in which they simply surrender to the status quo they are fighting against in exchange for good treatment. They need to participate in a conflict-resolution process that addresses the core issues. As the stronger party, you may be expected to make the first move. **Know your redlines.** A redline is only meaningful if you are willing to fight for it—which means your soldiers could be wounded or killed over it. Choose them carefully. If you establish a redline and then allow it to be crossed, you will lose credibility.

SCENARIO 5

Learning and Adapting

This time, I went back into the simulation without rewinding it. The Nar area was fairly peaceful by now. The councils at community and area levels were functioning well and making decisions. They provided good checks and balances with Bar Pak and the government.

We had made important inroads in the Mir and Zari areas but had hit a wall. Without some sort of change in approach, we were not going to move forward.

Learning and Adapting . . . Again

Bala Khan had too much popular support for us to make further progress in the Mir area. The people wanted an end to violence but did not want to see Bala Khan humiliated. From their perspective, he was fighting for legitimate and understandable reasons.

Meanwhile, Sher Wali and the Zari insurgents had adapted to our approach and begun a murder and intimidation campaign in the contested areas. I worried that we would lose ground unless the population could be mobilized and protected. They were not going to take our side in the near term, but we could work toward common objectives.

The Mirgul-area terrain was more accessible, and local governance worked there; it was just at odds with us and the government. Zari, on the other hand, was remote and inaccessible; governance and social cohesion were fractured to a greater extent. We could use more formal approaches in Mirgul. Zari required an unconventional method—securing just the main road would consume my entire battalion. I could not afford to do that—I would have to choose carefully if I decided deploy additional forces there.

Refining the Approach in Mirgul

Bala Khan was the head of the powerful Khosi clan of the Mir tribe. They were the dominant group in Mirgul and the surrounding villages. If I was to get Bala Khan into some sort of conflict-resolution process, I would need to build a relationship with people important to him. Naseem and I also had to get through to Bar Pak and Al'a Dust—they would need to be willing to put their feuds aside. I needed some leverage for that to happen.

We still did not have a proper council for Mirgul or the greater Mirgul area that would work with us. But we had enough inroads with enough people that word would eventually get back to Bala Khan and those closest to him. I had the sense that we had gained credibility with the people. They were now willing to explore some sort of way out of the conflict. As the most powerful party, we were expected to make the first move. But I had to do so while also having Bar Pak and Al'a Dust on board or the efforts would lack integrity.

Naseem and I discussed the way forward. We decided to begin at the bottom, using company- and platoon-level engagements to talk with community leaders and lower-level government and police officials. Bar Pak, Al'a Dust, and Bala Khan would all need some pressure from below. This effort would also give more visibility to the personal networks of each key actor—they were not monolithic, especially Bala Khan's network. We would need to use our hard-won credibility to play an honest broker role.

My subordinate leaders began asking people, community leaders, and lower-level government and police officials why people in the Mirgul area were fighting. The common answer was Markhand. That was a ready scapegoat, and an easy way for people to try to evade scrutiny of their communities and avoid addressing painful issues.

We pressed further. While agreeing that Markhand was a problem, we also observed to the community leaders that there was a certain pattern to the fighting. When the crops were being planted and harvested, the violence would drop to almost nothing. Between those times, violence picked up. We also had heard, on the militant walkie-talkies, fighters speaking the local dialect. Those coincidences surely could not be explained as Markhand's doing.

After a bit more probing and relationship building, we began to get more consistent and realistic answers. Bar Pak and Al'a Dust, the people claimed, had a feud with Bala Khan. This had started in the Markhand wars and the earlier insurgency against Archon. Al'a Dust and Bala Khan were both fighting for Khanastan independence against Archon and then against the Markhand invasion. Al'a Dust was told that Bala Khan had given information about him to the Markhand forces, who then came after Al'a Dust. They killed his wife and two oldest sons and nearly killed Al'a Dust. He had never forgiven Bala Khan and wanted revenge.

When Bar Pak became the governor after the war, Al'a Dust convinced him that Bala Khan was a tool of Markhand. So Bar Pak began taking action against Bala Khan and the Khosi clan. He took some of their prime farmland and sold it to his friends. He took money that was supposed to support the Khosi people for himself. He made sure any projects in the area failed (now I had new insight into the micro-hydro plant and the school that had collapsed in the earthquake in the previous scenario). In the past, he made such problems appear to be our fault—or at least done with our complicity.

He and Al'a Dust convinced the coalition that Bala Khan needed to be killed or captured. The special forces came after him over a year ago, searching his house and many others in Mirgul. Firefights broke out in the village, and many civilians were killed. Women said that jewelry was stolen from their houses. All felt humiliated by the intrusion: the bags over the heads of innocent people, the treatment of all as guilty of crimes they could not understand and never committed. The timber mill, which Bala Khan owned and which provided many jobs to people in Mirgul, was destroyed. Those are the reasons why the violence here began, the people said.

Bar Pak and Al'a Dust deliberately split the Mir to weaken the tribe and undermine Bala Khan. They befriended the smaller Merk and Gork clans, who mostly lived in the Nargul area, giving them money and support in return for their allegiance. They were at war with the Khosi clan, which was supported by the Suk. The Qala clan, meanwhile, was a weaker and marginalized clan of the Nar tribe and often supported Bala Khan. Until these kinds of issues were addressed, the people said, no peace could come to the area.

A Different Adaptation in Zari

The situation in Zari was much different. Sher Wali had also fought Markhand. He began as an ordinary fighter from the Bamal clan and rose through the ranks over time to cell leadership, and then on to more responsibility. He played a key role in financing the militant network through smuggling and other black market operations.

He also grew to become a religious zealot, straying from the moderate Jamma Rhun school and toward a puritanical Domol-like ideology, meting out rough punishments to people under his control who violated the norms of his extremist sect.

Very few of the Zari people supported his extreme views. Nonetheless, Sher Wali was an effective commander and financier during the Markhand conflict. The people overlooked his methods at the time, believing they would be able to control him after the war was over.

The primary Zari-Sattar insurgent leader in Zari at the time of the Archon insurgency and Markhand invasion was Akhtar Gul, who was from the Salar clan—the largest Zari clan and the one in control of Zargram. He was powerful and beloved enough to unite the tribe. He was a brilliant tactician, was fair and honest with money, and solved disputes with wisdom and justice. He died mysteriously at the end of the war. Some believed he was poisoned by Markhand operatives, others thought he was murdered by the rival Bamal clan, who sought an upper hand in tribal politics.

After Akhtar Gul's death, the Zari tribe fractured between the Salar and Bamal clans, with the weaker Zargot and Kala clans alternating sides opportunistically. Sher Wali gained the most through all of the infighting. He asserted control of the northeastern valleys, while the Salar controlled Zargram and the villages along the river.

The Bamal, however, were not monolithic in their support for Sher Wali and his puritanical rules. They feared a tribal war with the Salar over the death of Akhtar Gul, which made most of them prefer clan cohesion, even if that meant living under Sher Wali's rules.

I also learned that relationships did not always align cleanly with clan affiliation. Business and personal interests also played important roles. Sher Wali had business relationships with members of the Salar clan, who would deftly play off their clan and business relationships to maintain ties with both groups. Threats to business interests could trump clan interests. The extent to which foreign forces could be scapegoated as threats enabled these individuals to maintain plausible affiliations with both groups.

Different Ways to Make and Measure Progress

I was surprised at how little we really knew about Bala Khan's or Sher Wali's networks. We generally knew the names of their subordinate leaders, but little about their backgrounds and motivations. Before, we really did not care about this or think to ask the questions. The prevailing assumption had always been that insurgents were irreconcilable enemies who had to surrender or be killed or captured. They had no other way out.

The no-way-out perception, ironically, worked to the insurgents' advantage. Once someone was labeled an insurgent—or believed he was labeled an insurgent—he also was convinced that he had no way out. Few in this culture would simply surrender and leave their fate to corrupt officials, or to indefinite confinement in one of our detention centers. Some would leave the area. Many others began actively or passively supporting Bala Khan or Sher Wali for the sake of protection or retribution.

We had to develop a better understanding of the relationships and motivations of various leaders within the networks. We needed to ascertain the extent to which they were reconcilable or not, what motivations were most compelling to them, and the nature and strength of their relationships with others in the network. We also had to develop ways to test and verify our assessments. Because relationships and intentions were often dynamic, we needed to monitor changes as well.

We also needed a more reliable way to measure progress. Before, we had used various input and outputs metrics—number of police and government officials trained, number of insurgents killed, number of projects and amount of money spent, and so on. This was all important to know, but it could be very misleading in terms of measuring meaningful progress toward defeating the insurgency.

Simply training more police or officials without addressing predatory corruption, abuse of power, and social exclusion—all issues that helped fuel the insurgency—more often than not meant we had merely added more capably corrupt police and officials.

The number of insurgents killed was meaningless as long as the issues that made insurgency attractive remained unaddressed. The militants simply regenerated in greater numbers.

The number of projects and amount of money spent were misleading as well. More money could simply mean more opportunities for corruption. Projects that were poorly built or lacked popular ownership often caused more problems than they sought to solve.

Naseem and I discussed how we could measure progress more effectively. Based on his experience, he suggested we look not just at violence levels but also community governance and cohesion, freedom of movement, and prices of goods.

We came to the conclusion that we had to measure progress toward defeating the insurgency through four interlocking filters. First, we needed to know whether levels of violence were increasing or decreasing. We measured the number of incidents, the intensity of them, who was initiating them, and the trend lines. Sporadic, ineffective direct- or indirect-fire attacks required few resources and little popular support. IEDs required a network of people—logisticians, technical experts, emplacers, and security. They also required cache locations. These operations required more popular support than did direct-fire attacks. Large-scale attacks or complex direct-fire and IED attacks required significant popular support. Because most insurgents operated within a finite distance from their community, we could use these assessments to get greater fidelity on the intensity of insurgent support in different areas.

Trend lines were also important. If we had experienced several large or complex attacks in a certain area and then the nature of the incidents changed to sporadic direct fire, that was a good indicator of eroding popular support for violence. If, however, we experienced sporadic direct-fire attacks and then the intensity grew to IEDs and complex attacks, popular support for insurgency was probably increasing.

Especially when we were new to an area, we needed to carefully cultivate public support and resist acting on early HUMINT reports. Having the patience to understand the environment would help us ensure that we acted on the right targets and did not wind up in the middle of somebody's blood feud. Doing that while addressing grievances and other "root cause" issues prevented low-level attacks from becoming a gateway to IEDs and larger incidents.

We paid particular attention to violence and intimidation against civilians. In the past, we had measured only attacks against our forces, which limited our understanding of the more important social and political control efforts of insurgent leaders like Sher Wali. Violence against us was often used by them to mask population-control efforts—keeping us focused on our own protection. They also used violence against us in attempts to provoke overreactions and civilian casualties in areas where they were trying to gain popular support. To get a better sense of public safety and security, we used feedback from sources such as local surveys and routine interactions with the people, freedom of movement, and frequency of invitations to villages and council meetings.

Assessing the degree of local versus external fighters served as another indicator of popular consensus. A high percentage of local fighters meant popular support or acceptance of insurgency was critically high—people were willing to have their sons and daughters fight, and die, against us. A high percentage of outsiders indicated less popular support. In some cases, people accepted insurgency but preferred the fighting be done by others; in other cases, the fighting was exported from one community area to another against the will of the people. The latter case suggested lack of cohesion and strength within the unwilling community—they were unable to prevent the encroachment.

Second, we measured the effectiveness of local governance mechanisms and access to villages. If a community had a functioning council that met with us and the government routinely, which we visited frequently, and that played an active role in governance, decision making, and dispute resolution, that was an indicator that the council was in charge and supportive. The absence of those indicators meant the community was contested or under the control of the insurgents. Cross-referencing these indicators with violence data gave us a better picture of whether violence in the area was local or from adjacent or external areas. If a community area experienced little violence itself but lacked the governance and access indicators, that generally meant that the community was exporting violence to another area, or permitting the movement of fighters through the area.

Third, we looked at freedom of movement—Would people travel from one community to another? Go back and forth to and from markets in the main villages? What were the lines of "flow" along the roads? Biometric data came in very handy for this assessment. A road traveled frequently by families generally meant security was good. A road traveled only by pickup trucks hauling large quantities of goods often indicated security was poor. One person would have to run the gauntlet, so to speak, to bring foodstuffs and other items to the community, often paying bribes along the way. Lines of flow indicated where people believed the roads were safe or insecure. A community from one tribe that chose to shop at the bazaar of a village from a different tribe and avoid the bazaar of it own tribe often indicated which parts of a main road were safe and which parts were not.

Of course, in some cases the people were free to travel, but insurgents would attack only us or the police. The extent to which people traveled in proximity to our patrols was an indicator of whether this dynamic was at work. We used to use "escalation of force" procedures and warnings to keep people far away from our patrols because of the suicide bomber threat. We changed this approach, permitting people to travel relatively close while keenly watching for behavior that suggested suicide bombing intent. First of all, suicide bombings were quite rare. Second, the better we built relationships with people, the more they took ownership of our protection. As we built relationships, I generally felt much safer in a crowd than in a deserted area.

Finally, we measured the prices of goods. The price of food in an insecure area was much higher than in a secure one. People would need to pay bribes at illegal checkpoints and to corrupt police, and the transporters would charge much higher fees due to risk. A bag of wheat in Zargram, for instance, cost five times more than the same bag in Nargul. So even if an area had little overt violence, high costs of goods indicated insurgent control or significant threat. An area of relatively high violence but low cost of goods and good freedom of movement indicated insurgent control and popular support.

These interlocking filters gave us a meaningful assessment of security and stability and the extent of insurgent control. No set of measures is perfect, but these "outcome" metrics enabled us to evaluate the effectiveness of our operations far more reliably than the input and output data.

The Mirgul area was clearly under Bala Khan's control—it had high degrees of intense violence against us, no functioning representative council that would work with us and the government, good freedom of movement for the people to and from Mirgul, and relatively low price of goods. Rarely would people travel between Mirgul and Nargul. They were physically connected by a road but not connected by commerce or movement of people.

The Zari area was contested by Sher Wali. Although Zargram was relatively friendly, as were Nishigram and other villages along the valley that were dominated by the Salar clan, the price of goods in Zargram was extraordinary. No area council existed. Pickup trucks carried large quantities of goods between villages. The Zargram elders could travel freely—Sher Wali did not want to start a tribal war—but goods were "taxed" at road tolls by Sher Wali's men. People complained about the tolls, but the Salar elders also did not want a tribal war and were not strong enough to demand and enforce an end to the illegal checkpoints. People from Nishigram would travel to Nargul rather than Zargram to trade and buy goods.

Building Connections

To develop a better understanding of Bala Khan's network, we began building relationships with people in surrounding villages and on the outskirts of Mirgul. I wanted to find people who had influence with Bala Khan. The older men were often the best sources of information. Few of them had personal agendas, and they valued the fact that I wanted to listen and learn from them. Our female engagement teams also proved instrumental in this effort. Over time, they were able to communicate key messages to Bala Khan's network and to receive messages back. They helped us to determine some of the major friction points and assess which themes were resonating and which were not.

At the recommendation of the FETs, Naseem and I met Saki Gul, an elder from the village of Balrok. He must have been in his sixties. He looked to us as if he were in his late eighties—because of hard living, adults over thirty often looked twenty years older than their age. Saki Gul had been a schoolteacher in Mirgul and had known Bala Khan since he was young. When Bala Khan was eleven, his father was killed by Archon security forces. Saki Gul grew closer to him and his brothers, often taking care of them when necessary.

When Bala Khan grew older, he gave Saki Gul a family house in Balrok and a nice plot of land. As we learned from the FET, Saki Gul's daughters had married into Bala Khan's family. His son, Hamid Gul, was an insurgent leader for Bala Khan. He did not know for sure that I knew all of this.

I told Saki Gul that I wanted to learn more about the Mir and why they were so upset with the government.

"I am too old for war now," Saki Gul told me. "My son is in the mountains. He was driven away by the government." Going into the mountains was code for being an insurgent. Being driven away by the government was also a veiled way of saying that he was fighting against us as supporters of the government. Saki Gul said he had not seen his son for over a year but had gotten messages from him that he was doing well.

I explained to Saki Gul why we were here, emphasizing the importance we placed on education and how we wanted to help the children.

"We have a lost generation of young men and women," Saki Gul said. "During the wars with Archon and Markhand, we could not continue school. Our enemies would target schools and other places where children gathered. This was a way of ethnic cleansing—destroy the youth. Most of our teenagers joined in the fighting, my son included. The younger boys and girls stayed at home, helping their families until they were old enough to fight. Most members of my tribe from ages ten to thirty are uneducated. Our society is collapsing.

"We thought that gaining independence from Archon and throwing out the Markhand invaders would bring peace and we could resume education. Then the government came and began persecuting us again. That is when our young people returned to the mountains."

"Why does the government persecute the Mir?" I asked.

"Not all of the Mir are persecuted. The Merk clan lives mostly in Nargul area now, so do many Gork. It is the Khosi and Suk that are persecuted. The Khosi is the biggest and most educated clan of the Mir tribe. I am Khosi.

"Bala Khan and Al'a Dust were good friends throughout the wars. They were the best commanders and worked together well for the people. Toward the end of the Markhand wars, someone tried to murder Al'a Dust. They killed his wife and two sons. Al'a Dust was nearly killed and walks with a limp now. Bala Khan was blamed for the attack. That is why the government persecutes the Mir."

"Did Bala Khan try to kill Al'a Dust?" I inquired.

"No. Bala Khan is a good man. He would not do such a thing."

I probed a bit further. "Who do you think did it, then?"

"I do not know," he said. "Maybe Markhand intelligence forces."

"But doesn't Bala Khan now get support from Markhand?"

"He may get support from kinsmen in Markhand," said Saki Gul. "One way for Markhand to keep the people weak here is to make them fight each other. It would not at all be uncommon for Markhand to attack Al'a Dust, blame Bala Khan, and then provide support for Bala Khan to defend himself against Al'a Dust while also professing support for the Khanastan government. That is how things work here."

This was very interesting to me. "If Bala Khan was not responsible for the attack on Al'a Dust, then why didn't he say so?"

"Because Al'a Dust is convinced Bala Khan did this. If Bala Khan tried to meet Al'a Dust to explain, then he would be approaching him as one who was apologizing for the attack and asking forgiveness. Since he was not responsible, Bala Khan will not apologize."

I repeated back to Saki Gul what I thought he had said. Naseem confirmed that I had it about right. As I was talking, Saki Gul was nodding. As I had suspected, Saki Gul understood English very well. I needed to use this to my advantage.

I asked him to teach me. "In your culture, how would these kinds of problems get solved?"

"The council would investigate and solve the dispute," said Saki Gul. "Now we have no real provincial council. Our society has collapsed into warring factions. The Nar and Mir now have enmity with each other because of the attack. This problem, of course, works to the advantage of the people who started the dispute in the first place. It also works for the Nar because the government supports them. The Mir are the ones who are without support. I fear for my tribe."

"One thing that is still unclear to me," I said, "is if the Markhand intelligence forces did this, how did the Markhand get enough information to find Al'a Dust? Surely the people would not simply tell them where Al'a Dust and his family were living."

"I can speak no more of this," he said. "I am tired."

I turned to one of my officers and, within earshot of Saki Gul, I told him that I believed that Bala Khan had probably been framed for the attack on Al'a Dust. I believed Saki Gul that Bala Khan was a decent man who was fighting to preserve his tribe. We had been given bad information about Bala Khan. We needed to help the Mir. They were not our enemies.

I asked Saki Gul if we could meet again in a week. He agreed to do so. I hoped that in the meantime word of our conversation would get back to Bala Khan.

I did not yet know if Saki Gul's story was true or if he was just protecting Bala Khan. The story was plausible. The attack on Al'a Dust smelled like an inside job and a way to blame Bala Khan. Markhand certainly had an interest in fomenting strife in this border region, and I was certain that there were people in Narabad as well who had personal and financial interests in keeping the war going.

The next day Nassem and I met Afzal, another gray-bearded confidant, in his village of Popgul. I asked him what he knew about the dispute between Al'a Dust and Bala Khan. He gave an account similar to what Saki Gul had said. He believed that it was an inside job and that Bala Khan had been wrongly blamed. He also explained that Bala Khan had met Al'a Dust and his family the day before the attack, at the latter's home in Baba Gul. Al'a Dust was told that Bala Khan had reported the location of his home to Markhand intelligence. For Al'a Dust, even if it was not Bala Khan himself who gave the information but a member of his security team, Bala Khan was still culpable.

"If a member of Bala Khan's group betrayed Al'a Dust," said Afzal, "it was still Bala Khan's fault. He should have found the informant and executed him. Bala Khan has not done so. Therefore, Al'a Dust believes that he condoned the attack."

Zari was a different problem altogether, according to Afzal. Sher Wali was a bona fide bad guy who was aiming to control the Zari area of Narabad.

I asked him if he could tell me about Akhtar Gul and the circumstances of his death.

"I have less information about that. Akhtar Gul was also a good man. We knew each other, but not well. He was a wise leader and respected by all the Zari clans. He created the Zari-Sattar insurgent group. He was one of the few leaders able to bring the Salar and Bamal clans together. Sher Wali was one of his subordinates and was very good at getting resources for the Zari-Sattar in the Archon insurgency and Markhand war."

"Does Sher Wali have ties to Markhand?" I asked.

"I believe he does, but he claims to hate the Markhand and the government equally. He wants the Zari area to be independent and to live under his rules."

I probed further. "How do the Zari people feel about that?"

"The Zari are very independent people, but also very practical. They reject Sher Wali's religious views, but they are too fractured to unite against him."

"Do you believe Akhtar Gul was murdered?" I asked.

"I am not sure, but I do not think so," the old man replied. "Some people believe he was poisoned. He might have just been in bad health. He was always very red in the face and complained of fatigue and pains in his chest. I think he had a bad heart. Markhand operatives could not get to him, and the people loved him. Sher Wali's grief over Akhtar Gul's death turned him into a religious fanatic. I do not believe he was responsible either."

It would have been too good to be true if Sher Wali was responsible, I thought to myself.

Several other conversations with people in various villages and towns generally confirmed the accounts we'd gotten from Saki Gul and

Afzal. I was relatively convinced that Bala Khan was reconcilable, but Sher Wali was not. Further study of their networks and subordinate leaders gave us an initial assessment of where those individuals existed on the reconcilable spectrum.

Most of Bala Khan's fighters were tribally rather than ideologically motivated. Sher Wali's network was more complex—a mix of tribal, financial, and ideological interests. We would need to influence Bala Khan to sway his organization, and the Mir tribe, decisively. We had to work from the bottom up and with local Zari leaders to undermine Sher Wali's network.

Another Meeting with Saki Gul

Naseem and I met a week later, as planned, with Saki Gul. I began by asking him how we could work toward peace in the Mirgul area.

"First, you need to work with the council. The Mir people need to be supported."

"I thought there was no council in Mirgul," I replied.

"Of course Mirgul has a council," he said. "That is how we maintain order. They just are not willing to meet with you and the government. That is why you thought they did not exist."

Okay, that was an important insight and made sense to me. "How can I meet with them?"

"You need to make a gesture of sincerity that is meaningful to them. Your previous attempts to do things for the Mir people were seen as an attempt to split them apart or fool them with bad and unsafe projects. And they will not trust anything if the government is involved."

"What matters to the people?" I asked.

"We want education for our children and jobs for our people. We want to be left alone by the government and to control our own affairs. Most of our children have no school; they meet in a barn or under a blanket outside. They have nothing to write with except a lone chalkboard. They have to use a limestone because there is no chalk. Or they write in the dirt with a stick."

I repeated back to make sure I understood his point. "What should happen after working with the council?"

"The council will try to convince Bala Khan to stop fighting you if they agree you are sincere. A few months ago, a bomb exploded near one of your vehicles and killed and wounded some children in Balrok. One of your soldiers told me that he wanted to help the people, but then he left once your people were taken care of. You will need to overcome these kinds of insincerities."

I recalled the IED explosion in Balrok in the second scenario; apparently a similar incident had taken place in the background in this simulation as well. I rememberd the pleas of the patrol leader to stay and assist and regretted my foolishness and impatience.

"Your recent work in reaching out to the people has not gone unnoticed," said Saki Gul. "But people are unsure whether this is genuine or an attempt to split us apart. We have a saying that a hundred good deeds are undone by one bad deed. But do not expect peace until the problem between Bala Khan and Al'a Dust is resolved."

And we have a saying that one thousand atta-boys does not equal one aw-shit, I thought. We had a lot of aw-shits to overcome.

"So the council and Bala Khan might be willing to work with us, eventually, but the government is another matter," I summarized.

"The council could be convinced that you were given bad advice if they think you are sincere. That disagreement can be resolved more easily than the one with Al'a Dust."

I would have to think over his advice and come up with a plan. "No one wins through the violence except for the people who are profiting from the violence itself," I remarked.

He nodded in agreement. "If the only choice is fight with pride or surrender in shame, people will fight. If, however, they are offered a dignified way to resolve a conflict, they will begin to doubt the wisdom of fighting."

Naseem asked about education and how we could assist the people. I told Saki Gul that I believed, as he and Naseem did, that education is the greatest gift one generation can give to another. "We have a lot of school supplies sent to me by families in America to support children's education. How could we get them to the children?"

"The people will not allow outsiders near schools," replied Saki Gul. "I am sure you can understand that, based on our experience with

Archon and Markhand. However, I could meet you on the south end of the Mirgul bazaar. We will get the supplies to the children."

Naseem explained that we could get the supplies there in two days. I asked how I could meet with members of the council.

"You have already met one." Saki Gul smiled. "Let us take this one step at a time."

We parted company with Saki Gul. I wondered if he was sent deliberately by the Mirgul council or whether he was doing this on his own initiative. Nonetheless, we had an opening that might come to nothing or could lead toward stability in Mirgul. Education was a way to establish some common ground and build trust. All of the work we had done to engage with the people just might start paying off.

Two days later, we met Saki Gul and two younger men at the south end of the bazaar. We had two trucks loaded with school supplies—far more than he had expected. The two men had been planning to carry the supplies themselves, in the traditional way of wrapping items in a blanket and slinging them over the shoulder, but soon realized that was not feasible. Saki Gul directed one of the men to get a pickup truck. The two men carefully loaded the boxes into the back.

"You are very generous, commander. We had not expected so much."

He had told me that the school had about two hundred children; we wanted to be sure we had enough. I knew that he would not open the box in front of me, as that would be rude in his culture. I opened two of the boxes and showed the notebooks and pens and pencils and asked if those were useful for the children.

Saki Gul's eyes lit up, "Yes, that is perfect. Our children have not had these for years. They will be very thankful."

I was not sure how this gesture would be received, but I was cautiously optimistic it might open further doors—and minds—in Mirgul.

Honoring the Dead

Naseem and I returned to the Nargul outpost. We had grown closer over time and began to share stories about our past. I wanted to learn more about his time in the Markhand wars and about his family. I thought that at this point in our relationship I could finally broach these subjects.

"My wife was a beautiful Torag woman from a powerful family of a neighboring village. Our parents arranged the marriage. I never saw her until our wedding day. We fell in love at first sight," Naseem replied.

"Does that happen often . . . parents arranging a marriage and the two people falling in love?" I asked.

"On the first part, yes—parents often arrange the first marriage," Naseem replied. "These arrangements are normally about status and tribal relations. Sometimes they fall in love, but mostly not. This is part of the reason some men take second wives. The first is for status and to respect their parents, the second is for love . . . the connection of soulmates. We were lucky that our souls connected."

"Does she have anything to do with the tattoo on your left arm?"

"Yes, they are letters in my language; representing the words she spoke when we knew we were in love."

"May I ask what those words were?"

"I like your face," Naseem replied, tears welling up in his eyes. "She always knew just what to say . . . words that would stir my soul."

"What happened to her?" I asked.

Naseem looked off into the distance. "Our village was massacred by Markhand forces during the war. My groups had joined up with those of my friend and mentor, Abdul Amin, to attack Markhand forces in an important district. We annihilated them. Other Markhand units took revenge and razed my village before we returned. I found the burned corpses of my wife and two children in a mass grave."

He told me more about his family and his village. I could tell that the memories were difficult, but that he was at peace. "I reburied them near our home and planted blue and white hydrangeas and lilies of the valley over their grave. Hydrangeas were her favorites; lilies of the valley are symbols of love to us."

"My wife taught me about the value of friendship," Naseem continued, "that true friends change one another for the better, especially when the change is difficult. Even in the most challenging times, she focused on the positive. She said that the calling of every person is to bring out the best in others, to make the world a better place."

He continued after a long pause. "She taught me that the only life worth living was one in which we make the most of every moment and every relationship; that we must keep faith with ourselves and our values and not settle for less. She believed that leading a life of regret and missed opportunities was a betrayal of oneself and others. And she believed that we must not allow important things to be left unsaid—life can be too easily lost or taken away. That is also how she raised our children."

We sat in silence, each reflecting on what Naseem had just said.

I then asked about Abdul Amin.

Naseem smiled. "Abdul Amin was the commander of the Torag tribal forces. No one was more feared by Markhand than him." Naseem went on to recount various battles and how Abdul Amin mastered his enemies. He died in the last battle of the war in the Torag area.

Naseem leaned forward to me with his arms outstretched and palms upward, as if pleading. "What I learned most from Abdul Amin," he said, "was to be the reluctant warrior. Abdul Amin would always try to solve problems through diplomacy and negotiation first. He would offer every reasonable opportunity to solve problems peacefully before he resorted to violence."

"Didn't his enemies take advantage of that?" I asked.

Naseem's eyes lit up. "Of course—and that is exactly what Abdul Amin was counting on! Most of the time differences were reconciled peacefully, and war was avoided. The true enemies, however, would prove to everyone that they could not be trusted; that war was the only way to stop them. Abdul Amin never had problems raising forces."

"Didn't that approach frustrate his soldiers?"

"Quite the opposite," Naseem replied. "It reinforced the faith the soldiers had in Abdul Amin. By giving a foe the opportunity to choose peace, Abdul Amin showed his soldiers that he did not send them into battle lightly—that he valued their lives and well-being—and that when it came time to fight, all other reasonable choices had been explored. His soldiers went into battle willingly and proudly."

"All of that fighting must have been difficult for the soldiers—mentally, I mean," I said.

"Yes, indeed," said Naseem. "Abdul Amin would gather everyone together after the fighting and had soldiers from each group tell their stories and the stories of the dead. Everyone had to talk. The stories helped people understand what went on around them; helped them come to peace with the sacrifices of their friends.

"This ritual and the knowledge that fighting was the only reasonable alternative kept up the spirit of our soldiers. Very few succumbed to what you call post-traumatic stress."

Naseem continued, "People had faith in Abdul Amin, and Abdul Amin kept faith with them and with the dead."

"How did he do that?" I inquired.

Naseem replied, "He had the wisdom of knowing when he could achieve his aims without fighting and when he could not. No enemy was, as you say, 'irreconcilable' by nature—Abdul Amin made him show his true colors. He kept faith with the dead and with the living by not needlessly sending more to join them.

"He also kept faith with the dead by telling their stories, much as I am doing now," said Naseem. "We must not allow them to fall forever silent. Abdul Amin insisted that telling their stories is what keeps their legacy alive and passed forward to others. So, even when the stories are long forgotten, their spirit still lives in the spirits of others."

"That's beautiful," I said. "I wish I could have met your wife and Abdul Amin in person, but I am glad that I have now met them in spirit."

Naseem smiled. And at that moment, Naseem and I went from being comrades to being friends.

Meeting the Mirgul Council

Three days later, Saki Gul arrived at the main outpost with ten other elders, requesting to meet with Naseem Hazan and me. I told him that this was an unexpected but pleasant surprise.

"Our children asked us to thank you."

Saki Gul opened an envelope containing about a hundred thank-you notes written by the children using the paper and pens we had given them.

I told him that this was a great honor to be visited by elders from Mirgul and to receive the thank-you letters. Naseem commented upon how beautifully the children wrote.

"They spent a lot of time working on these letters. They are not used to writing with pens, so they often needed a few drafts. The other children are thankful as well, but they did not believe their handwriting was good enough for a letter to you."

I said how gratified I was by the kindness and thoughtfulness of the children, and I hoped that we could continue to support their school. Since the hour was approaching midday, Naseem asked the elders to join us for a meal, to which they agreed.

We sat in a private room, eating and making polite conversation. I mentioned to my company commander and staff officer, within earshot of Saki Gul, how glad I was to finally meet elders from Mirgul and hoped this could lead to a better relationship and overcoming misunderstandings.

Once the meal was finished, we continued the conversation. I mentioned that I wanted to get their advice on how to work together for peace in the area. I was confident that some, if not all, of the ten elders were members of the council. This was another confidence-building measure on their part to gauge our sincerity and to determine if what Saki Gul had told them was true. The elders needed more than one assessment.

One of the elders explained how the government was at war with the Mir tribe and that the foreigners were their agents in destroying the Mir and their community. This was a classic "anchoring" strategy. One would lay out a number of grievances, politely, to see how we would respond. Simple acceptance of everything would indicate that they could push further. Some gentle pushback would gain more respect and would be an indicator that I was not going to be a pushover. One or two others would then play the role of reasonable interlocutors.

I listened carefully to his side of the story and repeated back the complaints he registered. Naseem said there were many misunderstandings that led to grievances on all sides—and all sides had shared in creating the situation we had today.

The elder then got more specific, explaining how foreigners had raided their homes and stolen their belongings and killed and injured their people.

I said that I understood how upset he and the people were about that event, which happened well before my soldiers arrived. I could not change the past, but I could commit to working together so that it would not happen again, if they were also willing to work together.

"All foreigners are the same to us. It does not matter that it was not you specifically. Your people did this and your people support the government that makes war on our people. Therefore, you are responsible. And you," he pointed to Naseem, "give bad information to the foreigners."

"Are all the people in Narabad and Khanastan the same?" I asked. "Should the people of Mirgul be held responsible for Sher Wali's actions?"

That was a bit of a gamble. I did not know how they felt about Sher Wali but was reasonably confident that they did not share his extreme views and did not support his notorious abuse of the population.

"I accept your point," he responded.

Saki Gul stepped in at that point and remarked that misunderstandings can lead good people to take actions that they would not take if they had full information. I had passed that test in their eyes—Saki Gul was now working toward common ground.

After some discussion and agreement on the point, I remarked how the elders have always been known for their wisdom and that they proved this once again. We need to address these misunderstandings and develop ways to prevent them from recurring.

One of the elders, Barak Din, breathed a heavy sigh—that was a signal that they had gotten what they wanted out of the meeting and were ready to go. It was also a signal that he was the guy in charge. Naseem offered more tea, which they politely declined, saying that they needed to return to their village. We agreed to meet again in one week to continue the conversation.

At Naseem's insistence, neither of us mentioned Bala Khan or Al'a Dust during the meeting. That would have been premature. We wanted to convey the message that we were open-minded. We accepted that mistakes and misunderstandings—rather than any of us personally—were responsible for the present situation. We would stand our ground in a discussion, but we wanted to open a channel to work through differences. They wanted roughly the same outcome.

We began a series of weekly meetings, and gradually the attendance expanded to include more elders. We used the same confidence-building methodology that had worked so well in other areas.

I also needed to find out more about Barak Din. He was clearly the senior elder in the room, but probably not one of the head elders—we were too early in the process for them to emerge. He began speaking more at the meetings over time, and everyone listened.

Naseem discovered that Barak Din was a second cousin of Bala Khan and one of the leaders of the Khosi clan. His opinion of how things were progressing would be critical. I also guessed that over time the main elders would begin coming to meetings, initially remaining in the background until they felt the time was right.

In the meantime, we also discussed ways forward in Mirgul with Bar Pak and Al'a Dust. At first, they were highly resistant to any outreach efforts. I mentioned that any serious economic development for the province required better security and proper representation from all of the major groups. And that it would be unfortunate if I had to report that government officials were not supporting the Khanastan president's efforts to bring peace to the country. Narabad had always been one of the most violent places in Khanastan, I pointed out; they would look like heroes if the area stabilized.

They were not happy but knew that I was not going to budge on the issue. We had built a sufficient relationship to work through disagreements, and they understood that my soldiers and I knew enough about the area that trying to use us as pawns was not going to work.

My strategy was to play an honest broker role to get the government and people of Mirgul to work together. Ultimately, that was the only way we would be successful. We needed to gain sufficient credibility with the Mirgul council that they would influence Bala Khan to stop fighting, and then work over time to get the council integrated into provincial governance. At some point, the dispute between Bala Khan and Al'a Dust would need to be addressed, but that would need to be resolved by the people and the government.

Entering the Red Zone: A Visit to Pitigram

Stability in Zari required a different approach. Our relationships with the people and various village councils began to strengthen, but we had a very difficult time gaining traction in the contested areas. We deliberately reached out to Bamal elders and those of other clans to chip away at Sher Wali's main base of support and avoid perceptions that we were on the side of the Salar.

We also discussed with all of the clans that greater economic support would require an area council. We could support individual community efforts, but nothing more until the Zari began coming together.

We began requesting to meet with the Pitigram council. We wanted to turn up the heat on Sher Wali in his home base. I also wanted to set conditions for an operation up there. If the council would not come to us, then we would go to them.

We also looked for opportunities to make some inroads with Jamma Rhun clerics. Sher Wali's version of the sect was extreme and perverted—more like Domol than Jamma Rhun. Most people and most Jamma Rhun clerics did not support his ideology.

We received a report that a Jamma Rhun cleric was preaching violence at a gathering in Dadmuk, a village along the river between Nishigram and Zargram that was at the mouth of the valley that wound north and east toward Pitigram. My company commander requested the Nishigram and Zargram elders to invite the religious leader to the Nishigram outpost.

After several requests and guarantees of safety, the religious leader, Abdul Watan, eventually agreed to come to the outpost under the escort of the elders. My company commander asked him about the Jamma Rhun school and how it differed from the Hambali and Domol schools. He spent several hours with him, listening to his perspectives and learning about his religion, explaining why we were in the area, the various projects we had coordinated with the people, and how we were working together with community councils on community priorities. Abdul Watan seemed to grasp most of the discussion. He was gratified that we were willing to spend so much time with him.

My company commander then escorted him to the road, where some of our soldiers, KNA, and police had established a checkpoint and were entering biometric data for passersby. He explained the biometric system and how it enabled us to learn the names of people and their villages. Our soldiers greeted several people by name.

My company commander explained to him that every hundredth person entered into the system received a goat. He asked Abdul Watan if he would agree to be entered. Abdul Watan assented.

Sure enough, he was the one hundredth entry. My company commander congratulated him and brought forward a goat. He took a picture of the group, with Abdul Watan holding the goat by a leash. He said he knew that, being a religious figure, Abdul Watan would make sure the goat fed people of Dadmuk. The KNA company commander then submitted the picture and a short story to the local weekly newspaper.

At the next weekly religious service, Abdul Watan explained to the congregation that the people should work with the Americans and the government to support their communities. Several events of this kind over the weeks and months helped us gain further inroads.

Nonetheless, our almost daily requests for a meeting with the Pitigram council continued to be met with silence.

I decided it was time to pay them a visit.

Pitigram was located along a valley that ran southwest toward the Narzam River and northeast toward a mountain pass on the Markhand border. Helicopter landing zones were scarce, but we found places suitable for blocking positions on either side of the village.

We sent a patrol to Dadmuk, at the elders' invitation, to capitalize on the emerging relationship with the village. The Zargram elders agreed to meet us there. I figured that our patrol to the village would trigger some militant movement from Pitigram toward Dadmuk and would make the high-risk landing zone outside the village less vulnerable.

The next evening we conducted the air assault, inserting the blocking positions and the engagement force outside the village itself.

The plan worked well. A group of militants had moved to a position outside Dadmuk to observe the activity and seek opportunities to ambush our patrol. The air assault operation triggered their movement back to Pitigram, but they were intercepted and annihilated by the southern blocking position. Another group of militants fled Pitigram to the north as we landed outside the village. They ran into our ambush from the northern blocking position.

The engagement force itself met no resistance. We stayed in a patrol base about five hundred meters south of the village and waited for someone to greet us and the police. The first day passed with no contact from the village, other than some curious looks from farmers.

Recognizing that the roads north and south of the village were blocked, another group of militants attempted to flee east over the mountains that evening. We spotted them with a UAV and targeted them with two five-hundred-pound laser-guided bombs.

On the second day, a farmer approached our patrol base carefully and asked what we wanted. We said we had sent several messages requesting to meet with the village council, but never received an answer. We thought, perhaps, that the distance may have been too far for them to travel, so we decided to make the trip ourselves.

The farmer smiled. "We were wondering when you would come."

An hour later, a group of men and women arrived and asked what we wanted. We gave them the same message that we had given the farmer earlier and asked to meet with the council.

A few hours later, members of the council arrived and asked what we wanted. We said that our requests for a meeting had gone unanswered so we decided to make the meeting easier for the elders. We wanted to work with them to find out how to coordinate on priorities for the community, as we had done for many other Zari communities. We never mentioned Sher Wali.

The elders were clearly unhappy and anxious about our presence but agreed to meet with us at the patrol base. They were not willing to invite us into the village.

The elders brought tea with them to the meeting. Some of the members were clearly suspicious and nervous about our presence. I asked the elders to tell me about their village and community and their key priorities.

An elder named Ghani served as the spokesman for the council. During the rounds of introductions, one of my staff officers carefully recorded the names and clans of the council members. I looked carefully at the seating arrangement and body language. I wanted to determine who were "first among equals." I knew that Ghani, as the spokesman, was not among the senior leadership, but was one of their trusted agents.

My staff officers and I narrowed down the likely candidates to three. During a break, I assigned a person for each of the three elders to carefully monitor their reactions to various subjects. Naseem Hazan's soldiers were experts at reading body language and had trained us well. We would compare notes to see how well we picked up on subtle signals.

Before getting into any "business," Naseem asked about various historic personalities of the Zari tribe and, in particular, ones from Pitigram. We wanted to signal that we were interested in them as people and to try to connect with their oral history. It was also a subtle attempt to have them recall happier times—times that were governed by community councils rather than Sher Wali's dictates.

This approach elicited positive reactions from the elders and opened up further dialogue. They discussed their historic independence, the fight against Archon and Markhand, their respect for Akhtar Gul, and the sense of unity they had achieved in difficult times.

Nassem Hazan asked whether the current times were considered happy or sad times for the people. That question elicited a very nervous reaction—several of the elders looked toward two elders in particular for a silent signal on how to respond. We had guessed who one of them might be, but missed the other. I had two body language watchers in reserve that were unassigned, and one of them immediately picked up the dynamic and began observing the other chief elder's behavior.

Ghani had gotten the silent guidance he needed and proceeded to explain that these were difficult times. The government was corrupt and did nothing for the people. The people could not sell their timber because the government had outlawed the trade. They had no schools for their children or jobs. External parties harmed the people (this was code for foreign forces and elements, as well as people from outside the community). They wanted to be left alone to govern themselves as they had done historically.

There were a number of contradictions that we wanted to explore, but that would have to be left for another time. We focused for the time being on the desire to work together to support the community. We reiterated that "mistakes and misunderstandings" had been made by many people and that we were interested in addressing those when the community was ready to do so.

The hour was getting late. The elders said they needed to return to their families but that we could stay in the area for as long as we liked. They did not, however, invite us to the village.

We exfiltrated the patrol base during the night and returned to the main FOB. We kept a UAV overhead to assess the reaction of the people the next day. Sure enough, the community held a large meeting to discuss the previous day's events.

Break

Alex paused the simulation at that point and asked if I needed a break. We were well into the evening. I was exhausted. I thought that we were moving in the right direction and did not need a readout and detailed after-action review. I wanted to play this scenario out.

Alex posed a few questions that he asked me to think about during the break:

How do we get the government on board with issues such as local governance councils, checks and balances, and reconciliation—all issues that will be needed for some sort of credible conflict resolution? How do we get the leverage to overcome powerful incentive structures that will resist such efforts?

The Zari are likely to continue to ask for tribal police—is there any way to make that work without it becoming a predatory militia?

How do you think your chain of command will respond? What will you do if they do not support your efforts?

How will you respond if elders or an insurgent leader ask for a ceasefire? How will you manage that and prevent spoiler activity from undermining your efforts?

Isolating and Defeating the Insurgencies

I returned to the simulation the next day.

The Zari Elders Take Ownership

The Zargram elders had been at work, holding meetings with other villages in the area. They were trying to organize their tribe and gain some stability and normalcy.

Naseem Hazam had been assisting the elders in their efforts for several weeks. He recommended to Bar Pak that he hold a large meeting with the Zari tribe in Zargram. Bar Pak, who had never visited the area, agreed to do so.

We developed a plan to support the event, offering to match funding that Bar Pak could obtain from the central government. In the past, we had been content to fund these kinds of events ourselves. This practice was unintentionally creating dependency. Our resources were much easier to obtain than funds from the central government. We needed to help make the government's fiscal system work for Narabad, and part of that was requiring Bar Pak and his officials to create a "demand signal" for the resources.

We eventually got the support and resources in place and scheduled the event. As badly as I wanted to be involved in the meeting, this needed to be an event for the Zari tribe to come together on solutions and ways ahead for their tribe. Our presence at the event would very likely restrict debate and discussion. There had been a number of raids into the Zari area prior to our arrival that created huge animosity among the people. We had gained a lot of credibility with the people over time, but they would need to come together to determine how they would deal with us—that would be an important part of the debate that would not occur if we were present.

The event lasted for three days; roughly eight hundred elders were in attendance. Both Naseem and Bar Pak were present for most of the meetings but had pledged that the discussions would remain secret. I did not ask them to break these confidences.

At the end of the third day, the elders held a large feast. The next morning, Naseem, Bar Pak, and five Zari elders visited me at the Nishigram outpost.

Naseem introduced Zama as the chief of the council. Zama was an elder in the Salar clan. He was a student and confidant of Akhtar Gul and one of his key subordinate leaders during the wars. I had never met with him before. His nephew had been killed in a commando raid a year ago, and I suspected Zama had supported the insurgency after that. He said that he was committed to peace in the Zari area.

Much of the debate over the course of the three days had centered on whether the people were willing to work together with us or not. The relationship building over the past several months and our discriminant use of force created subtle shifts in the balance of power away from Sher Wali and his network and toward the elders who advocated peace. This opened a way for the tribe to work with us.

"We have decided that we want peace in our area and have united the tribe for this purpose. The Zari elders have elected a one-hundred-member council to govern the area and put an end to the fighting. The council is made up of members from each village and clan based on their proportion of the population. The number one hundred is a holy number in our tradition. I have been elected as the chief of the council and these four are my executive committee."

He introduced them by name and continued.

"We have decided that the war against the government is over and that we will work with the foreign development team but not with the combat forces. You have shown yourself to be a friend of the Zari and good at development and assistance."

I must admit that this formulation was really puzzling. Had this happened in an earlier scenario I would have exploded in outrage and told Zama to pound sand—I was a combat leader, not an aid worker. Naseem gave me a look that said "just go with it; I will explain later."

I said that I was honored by the meeting and wanted to work with the council to support peace in the area. I asked what his plan for doing so was and how could we support it.

"We are responsible for security in the Zari tribal area. We will let you know if we need assistance."

I liked the idea—this was popular mobilization at its best. What was the plan? Would they convince Sher Wali and his leaders to stop fighting?

Zama looked at me with a smile as if he were educating a grandchild. "No, we are not powerful enough to do that yet. We will visit each village. We will convince the villagers and youth to stop fighting. Once they are convinced and enough of them agree with us, then we will have the power on our side to convince the leaders."

Interesting . . . a bottom-up strategy—erode the networks from below to shift the balance of power and then dictate terms to Sher Wali. "What happens if he refuses?" I asked next.

"We have traditional ways of handling these matters. Those that refuse will get kicked out of their villages and their houses will be burned. If they refuse to stop fighting even then, we will turn them over to the government."

"Should we then just wait for your call? How else can we assist?"

"This is our plan and we are in charge. We work for neither side. We will stop the violence between the government and the people. We need to be free to talk with everyone without fear of being targeted by you or accused by the fighters of compromising them. We are poor men, so we will need some support for food and transportation. We want to continue to work with you on projects for our people—our young people will need jobs. Finally, we will need tribal police."

I began to understand what they had in mind. They would be the honest brokers in the area and the mediators between both sides. They wanted to be seen as neutral judges and decision-makers. I could assist with the money, but I also wanted Bar Pak to match the funds and eventually take over the support. There was a risk here that they would be seen as paid agents of us, which would undermine their role.

We also needed to maintain economic support for locally owned and operated projects in the communities. These gave us a critical foothold and something the council could continue to leverage in support of the youth and demonstrate their credibility. I told him that I would need to think about the tribal police and that he would need to show Naseem and me a plan for how that would work.

"I will visit you at the Nargul base in three days so we can discuss these matters further." Zama and his team bid farewell and departed back to Zargram.

I asked Naseem for his thoughts.

"They have a good plan," he said. "We will need to support them carefully so they are seen as the power in the area."

"But what about the government?" I asked.

"One step at a time," Naseem replied. "The council needs to be in charge and be seen by the people as being in charge. That is the source of their power. We will need to conform to their wishes, within reason. As the relationship builds, they will become the voice of the people and work together with the government. This is very important."

I said that I was not comfortable with the tribal police idea. We did not need another armed group running around. How would we know whether these men were insurgents or good guys?

Naseem brought forward one of his senior noncommissioned officers, a man from Zaristan who was a religious leader from the Jamma Rhun school of Jamdali practiced by the Zari. He intended to use him as the primary interlocutor with the hundred-man council and advisor to the two of us on how to best work with them.

"Commander, you should always consider their demands and work with them. They need to be credible to their people; they have to be independent and be able to make demands on both sides."

Most of their requests seemed reasonable, I thought. We would continue to coordinate with them and keep working projects and other decisions with the community council and larger issues with the tribal council. I was not so comfortable with the tribal police. If they needed protection, I suggested, we could offer army and police to protect them.

"That is not acceptable to them and would make them look weak."

I did not understand that at all and asked him to explain it.

"If they make a ruling and some people reject it, then they need to be able to enforce their decrees. If they have to turn to an outside force, like the army or police, then they send the message that they do not have the support of their tribe."

"But how do we know these tribal police will not become another insurgent group or predatory militia?"

"In Zari tradition, we raise local forces called zarikai. Members of the zarikai are nominated by their representatives in the council and approved by the full council. It is a great honor to be selected as zarikai. All clans are represented in proportion to their size. The commanders are selected by the council and rotate among each clan. The zarikai is under the control of the council to defend their communities and enforce their decisions."

"That seems reasonable to me. Why don't they just do it?"

"They need the government's permission and your agreement. After the Markhand wars, the government and the foreigners ordered all of the groups to disarm. What happened was that the good people gave up their weapons and the bad people kept them."

Naseem said that he would take the matter up with Bar Pak and Al'a Dust. They had no police in the Zari area anyway, so this was a reasonable request. Zama needed to present his plan so we could all be certain traditional rules were followed and that we had a way to recognize them. Naseem was confident that the people had enough personal weapons for the zarikai.

"One more thing," the Zari NCO concluded. "You will need to do things that show the people that you respect the authority of the council. You will need to be seen to follow their rules as well. Do you have the courage and confidence to do that?"

This could be difficult. I supposed the council was operating in good faith, but simply following their rules could place my soldiers at high risk, especially if they demanded that we stay in our bases and not patrol. I was not willing to take that kind of risk.

"The trick," counseled Naseem, "is to negotiate with them on these rules. Capture in a formal document an agreement to do the things you are already doing and prohibit things you have already prohibited while maintaining the necessary flexibility. The people will believe the council gained these concessions from you—all you are doing is making an agreement to do what you already practice."

"I can do that," I said, "but why will this help?"

"By showing that you respect the wishes of the council and the people," Naseem replied, "you take the moral high ground and put pressure on Sher Wali and his supporters to do the same. If they also respect the wishes of the council, then they will ultimately have to give up the fight. If they don't follow the wishes of the council but you do, then the people will turn against them. Either way, this works to our advantage."

Genius. I was glad Naseem was on our side.

Three days later, Zama and his executive committee presented their plan for the zarikai. It looked just as the Zari NCO described it—each village and clan was represented, and the commanders rotated among them. The council was in charge of the force but needed to keep Bar Pak, Al'a Dust, and Naseem informed of its activities.

A communications system was also established. The zarikai was restricted to Zari areas only, and any movement of ten or more zarikai outside of their home village needed to be coordinated with the government. They also had special colored and infrared armbands that would identify them to us. We insisted that their weapons be registered with the police and that they get enrolled in the biometrics database and receive an identification card.

Those rules were acceptable to Zama. "Good. We will continue our activities and keep you informed. We insist that we be able to meet with any group and not be compromised."

We agreed to that and requested that the council keep us informed of their movements so we could avoid any misunderstandings. Zama was reluctant. He feared we would follow them and then target Sher Wali or one of his subordinates after a meeting concluded.

"We have trusted you with the zarikai," said Naseem. "You need to trust us that we will not undermine or compromise your efforts."

Zama nodded, "We are going to need to create a formal agreement."

"We will consider this," replied Naseem. "We need to meet with the council every two weeks, or more often as necessary." Zama agreed.

We agreed to meet with the full council in two weeks at the Nishigram base to discuss these matters further, register the zarikai, and give the council some time to do their business.

"Let us discuss this agreement," said Naseem. "We will need to create something in writing with the council that shows we are responding to their authority but that retains the freedom for us to do our jobs. Remember how we bargain. The council will ask for full control of everything. They expect us to demand full control. We need to determine where we have room for accommodation. They do not know the rules we have given to our soldiers, and most of those will be acceptable to them. We just need to arrive at that agreement—to do what we are doing now—through difficult negotiations."

I nodded in agreement.

"Also," Naseem continued, "do not be afraid to get into arguments with them. They expect it and will respect it. We need to hold them accountable for their side. The more we can make it look like we are negotiating difficult issues and allowing 'wins' for the council without undermining our flexibility, the more reasonable we look and the more powerful the council looks in the eyes of the people."

Naseem and I worked out our "gives"—essentially things we were already doing, or not doing, that we would agree to capture in writing. We did not search houses or religious centers without prior coordination with the elders (unless a threat existed). We also worked with community councils on projects and assistance and visits to villages. We would agree to those things, while insisting on the right to respond to any threat. We also wanted accountabilities built into any agreement. Getting the incentive structures right would be critical.

We wanted this process to take a while to unfold. We were going to work other matters, primarily local decision making, using issues such as projects and economic assistance to build a habit of governance and ownership. Starting small with the council and then ending up with a written agreement would add credibility to the process while strengthening this very important governance mechanism in the eyes of the people.

Our first few meetings with the hundred-man council involved relationship building, coordinating key priorities, and building trust and credibility.

The first meeting took place at the Nishigram base. Bar Pak, Al'a Dust, Naseem, and I met them just inside the front gate, making sure the entry procedures were well-rehearsed and streamlined to minimize any inconvenience while also sending the message that security was important. We gave each elder the traditional touch to the other's heart followed by a handshake. Although I had dealt with crowds that size several times before, I was amazed at the wave upon wave of elders—they just kept on coming. Overall, I think just over one hundred and twenty entered.

We introduced one another, starting with the Narabad officials, then Naseem and me and the elders. They all sat in their brightly colored robes on a set of large blankets we had spread over a concrete pad. The four of us sat next to Zama toward the front. We discussed briefly the idea of having a head table but thought it might send an unintended message of superiority.

We decided that for our part, Bar Pak would speak first to open the session and then invite a Zari religious leader to offer a prayer. Abdul Watan, the cleric from Dadmuk, gave the prayer. Bar Pak then invited Zama to speak. He introduced the council and discussed their key priorities—ending violence, government coordination with the council, education for the children, and jobs for their people.

A few others gave speeches—mostly elaborating on those points. One decried the violence and suffering of the Zari people, another that the government did nothing for them and that this was only their second time ever seeing Bar Pak. A teacher, Akhtar Halim, spoke about education. Other spoke about jobs and building the local economy.

Bar Pak answered each of their issues and complained that he had never been invited to the Zari area to work with them. Naseem and I spoke about the importance of the council and our commitment to work together with them.

Zama raised the idea of the zarikai and asked for the approval of the elders and of the government—to which all assented.

We agreed to meet again in one week to register the zarikai and coordinate a plan for humanitarian assistance and school supplies. The elders agreed to bring lists of necessary school supplies and of families in need of assistance and the type of assistance required.

After the official portion, we had a meal of goat, rice, beans, potatoes, and nuts. The four of us broke up and sat with different groups of elders during the meal. I was with Zama, Abdul Watan, and a dozen others. I asked Abdul Watan if he wanted to offer a blessing.

He looked at Zama, who nodded in agreement. "In America, you pray before the meal to offer thanks for the food," Zama quipped. "In Khanastan, we pray after the meal—in thanksgiving that we are still alive."

We had a good laugh at the joke and then discussed our families while we ate. During the conversation, I praised the legendary hospitality of the Zari people and mentioned how important it was for us to be good guests.

At that point, Akhtar Halim, who was in Naseem's group, turned around and said in perfect English, "You are a good guest!"

He moved to a seat next to me. "Ever since you and your soldiers came to our area you have been working with the people and the elders. This meeting today would not be possible without your hard work."

I thanked Akhtar Halim for his kindness while the elders seated with me nodded in agreement. I felt good about the relationships we had made but was still unsure whether the hundred-man council could deliver.

After the meal concluded and the elders returned to their villages, Bar Pak, Al'a Dust, Naseem, and I discussed the event and the way forward.

Bar Pak seemed very skeptical and concerned. "There were a lot of bad people here today; people who have supported Sher Wali and other fighters. I am not sure we should continue this." Al'a Dust nodded slightly but did not offer any comment.

"What is the alternative?" Naseem asked. "If some of these people had been supporting Sher Wali in the past or were still doing so, this effort is one way to communicate with them so they can begin to see that Sher Wali has been lying to them—and that his way leads only to more violence. I say we should invite more of them."

We agreed to see where the effort led, but Bar Pak was still uneasy. I was not sure at the time whether he genuinely believed the council was a sham or felt his power was being threatened.

Pushback From Above

I also ran into consistent resistance from my boss, the brigade commander. He was highly skeptical of the whole effort, thinking the council was just a delaying tactic by Sher Wali to keep us distracted while he gathered power. He was upset that we did not do a "deep clear" of Pitigram while we had the chance. A lost opportunity, he said. He thought the idea of zarikai was an outrage but knew that he could not stop it because it had government backing.

This disagreement was new territory for me. I had always prided myself on supporting my boss and pushing the envelope to implement his ideas and directives better than anyone else. Of course, this was a cyber-brigade commander and not the real thing, but I could not help but thinking the two were pretty close in nature—their perspectives were quite similar and arguments likely to be very consistent. This was becoming another moral dilemma that I had not yet faced. What do you do when you know you are doing the right thing but your boss is convinced of the opposite?

Tough Decisions

We met consistently with the Zari council. The zarikai registration went without incident, and we received routine updates about the activities of the council. They were doing exactly as they had discussed—going from village to village and getting their young men to stop fighting. The humanitarian assistance and school supplies coordination also went perfectly. We also discussed priority projects and began implementing them using our standard practice of local ownership. We were building real momentum.

We ran into a major problem after a few months with the location of a small hospital for the area. Up to this point, the projects had entailed fairly simple prioritization and coordination with a couple of villages. This project affected the entire Zari area, and many elders wanted the facility placed near their own village.

Bar Pak wanted the hospital located near the Nishigram base (the Nishigram elders supported this, too), but the elders from Zargram insisted that it should be near their village, which was the main village of the tribe. Elders from Pitigram wanted it near their village, which would be a problem for reasons of access as well as the likelihood of it becoming a medical facility for Sher Wali and his fighters.

We held several meetings in which this issue, among others, was discussed. But Zama always asked for more time because the council had not yet come to consensus. We were reaching the point at which we would lose the facility if we did not commit the funds.

I raised the issue at a meeting and noted the risk of losing funding. Naseem counseled me not to push the issue too hard out of fear that the council would fracture. I thought the relationship could handle a little more prodding over the hospital.

As soon as I raised the issue, a couple of comments were made by members of the group. Then a full-scale argument erupted of the kind I had never quite seen. Beards were wagging, fingers were pointing, faces were growing red.

At this point, Zama turned to me and said, "We need to go pray."

I learned quickly that "going to pray" was code for "we do not want to argue in front of you." The elders departed the base and went to the Nishigram religious center.

They came back after two hours and resumed their positions on the blankets. Exasperated, Zama looked at me and said, "We cannot decide this matter on our own. We have too many disagreements. We have decided that we will follow whatever decision you make."

Naseem and I traded glances—we immediately had the same thought. The council needed to solve this one itself, or it would begin punting all tough decisions to us. If it did not have ownership of this decision, or other tough decisions, it would not ensure proper implementation. This was a huge risk.

I politely informed the council of my decision: that this was their decision. They would have to live with the location of the hospital for many, many years—long after we were gone. I could not in good conscience make the decision. Naseem and I could offer points of consideration, but that was all.

The council again erupted into argument. I was genuinely worried that I had pushed them too far. Zama once again asked leave to go pray.

The council came back one hour later. Zama announced that they were unable to come to agreement over the hospital, and if that meant that they would lose funding for now then they accepted that consequence. He also announced the formation of a "development" committee that would be chaired by Akhtar Halim, of the Bamal clan, and would have representatives from each village and clan. As he read the names, each person stood up.

Zama said that they would inspect each project ongoing in the Zari area and report the status to the council and inform us if any projects were going poorly. They would determine the best location for the hospital, and their decision would be binding.

Naseem and I agreed that this was an outstanding result. It was another example of the council taking responsibility and implementing systems that could last beyond our time in the area.

Another important step that began unfolding was the invitations to various Zari villages for meetings. The full council would meet us at the Nishigram base, and then we would travel together to a village to hold the meeting. They would then escort us back. Naseem's soldiers and mine would be spread by squad over the column together with members of the zarikai. The squads remained close enough together for mutual support, and we had surveillance and fixed-wing aircraft over head. Other members of the zarikai took up positions on the road and on ridgelines overlooking the road.

I was always concerned during these movements; Naseem was less so. We both agreed that this was a good sign—and that the elders were guaranteeing our safety. Their growing confidence was also a sign of their increased control of the area.

Another sign was the significant decrease in violence in the area. Several of Sher Wali's less-committed subordinates signed agreements with the council that they would cease fighting and stop supporting Sher Wali. Others were kicked out of their village. Some took to hiding in mountain caves with small groups of supporters. Others fled to Pitigram or into Markhand. Sher Wali was losing his grip on the people rapidly. Food prices dropped in Zargram as illegal checkpoints and taxes became less frequent.

We began signing what became known as "Commitments of Mutual Support" with villages during these meetings. As in the planned agreement with the hundred-man council, these mutual commitments provided the ground rules for how we would interact with one another and always included mutual accountabilities.

We would continue to work out village- and community-related issues with the local council; they promised to ensure no one from their village was fighting, turn over to the government the names of anyone refusing to stop fighting, and take ownership of all projects and ensure each was built properly.

The council also divided their tribal area into village areas of responsibility. The village or community was responsible for security in the specified area. Any security incidents would cut off projects and humanitarian assistance until the perpetrators were identified and held accountable to the satisfaction of the council and the government—which was represented by the local KNA commander. To guard against violence from outsiders, or the excuse that local violence was perpetrated by outsiders, the village was responsible for reporting violence and movement of insurgents.

During a meeting and signing ceremony in Dadmuk, which was down the valley from Pitigram, an event occurred that tested the council and our agreement. All of the elders in the village and many young men and women turned out for the meeting and ceremony—probably five or six hundred people in all, plus the hundred-man council.

The Khanastan army company commander held a list of names and called them out to see if the individuals were in attendance. He did not say so, but we knew that they were reported to be insurgents. As he called the names, the individuals stood up, about twenty in all. Two of those were sitting about ten feet from Naseem and me. We had removed our body armor and had placed our weapons on the ground—I had rarely been as nervous as I was just then.

Most of the named individuals were present, and the meeting began in earnest after all the names had been read. We discussed each item of the commitment of mutual support, and all affirmed agreement to the stipulations.

As the signing ceremony began, a few shots were fired from just outside the village toward one of our joint observation posts that we had set up for security. Army, zarikai, and my soldiers manned each one.

My forces at the position were led by a newly promoted sergeant. Within the rules of engagement, he had every reason to unload machine gun and grenade fire in the direction of the shots, and to call in artillery or mortar support. He surmised, however, that these shots were deliberately designed to provoke a violent response from us. The enemy wanted to derail the agreement.

Coolly, he directed his designated marksman (an expert trained to use a longer-range rifle) to fire a couple of rounds at the area from which the shots came. He called up the company commander and informed him of the situation and his actions.

He acted perfectly. The elders looked up when they heard the shots. The KNA company commander notified the audience of what had happened. Everyone went back to business. The Dadmuk elders acknowledged that they would be under sanctions specified in the agreement.

After the meeting concluded and we departed, the Dadmuk council investigated the incident and determined who was responsible. They administered some traditional justice to the individuals and reported their actions to the hundred-man council. We were satisfied with the response and agreed to lift sanctions.

All of these tests and many more convinced Naseem and me that the hundred-man council was legitimate and capable of making and enforcing decisions. The almost nonexistent violence, the absence of illegal checkpoints, the drop in prices of goods, access to villages, and general freedom of movement all indicated that security was improving substantially.

Resistance to Peace

Sher Wali, the elders reported, had left for Markhand. The Pitigram elders increased their engagement with the hundred-man council and coordination with us.

Bar Pak, however, remained concerned about the council and what he perceived as a loss of personal influence in the area. Naseem had rightly concluded that Bar Pak had attempted to govern using a few cronies in the area who were completely ineffective—they were not even chosen to be members of the hundred-man council. Some were members of a village council. He was upset that these cronies were powerless, and that their powerlessness implied a lack of authority and loss of face on his part.

"There are many bad people among the council. I am not convinced they truly support the government. At best, they support themselves and their people. I am considering whether we should continue working with them."

Naseem countered, "When one reconciles with former enemies, one has turned adversaries into friends. I count that as a blessing and a tribute to your leadership."

Bar Pak seemed to accept this but pulled me aside confidentially before he left and asked if I thought he was a good leader. I told him that I thought a good leader was one who could increase the number of people supporting him while he made tough decisions. A wise leader also knows how to govern through other people so they feel they own the results. As the ancient Chinese philosopher Lao-Tzu said, "they feel as though they had accomplished all of this themselves."

After Bar Pak took his leave, Naseem said that getting him to work with and through the Zari elders was relatively easy compared to the Mir elders. "His personal and financial interests in the Zari area are far smaller than in the Mir area. That will be the real test. It will also force him to deal with the dispute between Al'a Dust and Bala Khan—something he has been able to avoid until now. I am concerned about the next step."

Interest in our Efforts in Mirgul

The work with the Mir elders had been going better than expected. The relationship we built with Saki Gul had opened the door to working with the Mir tribal council. Skepticism was significant on both sides, but gradual confidence-building measures led to increased trust. Nassem and I were now meeting routinely with the Mir council. We needed to begin getting Bar Pak on board and, eventually, Al'a Dust.

Naseem and I made clear to the elders that we had no quarrel with Bala Khan. We recognized that mistakes and misunderstandings had led to the current state of affairs, which had harmed the Mir tribe the most. When the time was right, we would like to meet with Bala Khan.

The Mir elders agreed that we would need to get to that point eventually but that now was not the time. Bala Khan, they said, was in Markhand, waiting to see if these efforts were genuine.

Meanwhile, we had been tracking a cell phone that we believed, but could not prove, was associated with Bala Khan. The cell phone would go active at various times, particularly just before and soon after we were having meetings with the Mir council. We had asked repeatedly if any new personalities were in Mirgul. The elders always denied it.

I was confident the cell phone belonged to Bala Khan or one of his close associates. I believed that Bala Khan was monitoring the situation closely to determine whether our efforts were genuine or a trap.

Saki Gul requested a meeting with Naseem and me at his compound. We agreed to do so, but only if we could bring some local security with us to remain outside the compound. They would occupy checkpoints at nearby intersections. Although I was confident Saki Gul was true to his word about our security in his home, I was concerned about "spoiler" activity by others. Saki Gul agreed to the arrangement.

His wife had prepared a very nice meal for us. As we sat and talked afterward, Saki Gul said that he wanted us to meet more of his family. At that point, Hamid Gul entered. He was about thirty years old with a long but neatly trimmed beard and powerful build.

Naseem and I both stood and rendered the traditional greeting to Hamid Gul. He sat down next to his father.

"I wanted you to meet my son, who has returned recently from the mountains." Saki Gul was using the "code"—he did not want to implicate his son directly or confirm Hamid Gul's participation in the insurgency.

We took the hint and told Hamid Gul what a pleasure it was to finally meet him.

"I appreciate your kindness to my father," he said carefully. "In our culture, kindness to elders brings kindness to oneself."

And Naseem answered, "Yes, and the latest fish drawn from the river is the freshest," meaning that new beginnings are always possible.

We discussed with Hamid Gul the work we had done in support of children's education and the coordination with the council on their priorities for the people in the Mirgul area. We had hoped the recent absence of violence in the area would continue so we could keep supporting the people.

Hamid Gul answered that his father had told him of this work and that he was delighted to see the truth of it firsthand. "Many people are interested in the new developments and what this might mean for the future of our community."

Naseem said that the future was good and that now was the time for old adversaries to put away their differences and work together for the people. "The only ones benefitting from violence," he explained, "were those few profiting by it. We need to recognize these people for who they are and not allow them to destroy the future."

Hamid Gul agreed, "There are people on all sides profiting from the violence. The government is trying to exact their revenge while destroying the tribe. If they were honest, they would see that allegations of old wrongs are falsehoods."

"Indeed," replied Naseem, "but old grievances are hard to overcome unless new information comes to light that is worth considering."

"All information is not what it seems," observed Hamid Gul.

I interjected that information can be interpreted in different ways, and that accurate interpretations were important in shining light on old mysteries.

Hamid Gul agreed and then changed the subject to his desire to settle down and raise a family. "I hope my children live to see happier days than we have."

We departed soon afterward as the evening was getting late. We agreed to meet again. "When people stop dining together their aims grow apart," said Hamid Gul, quoting a Mir proverb.

We had built sufficient credibility with the Mir council to attempt to begin the process of reconciliation with Bar Pak and eventually with Al'a Dust.

Bar Pak agreed to meet with the Mir council at the Mirgul outpost. The meeting was cordial, but Bar Pak was cool to the elders. I was not sure if this was him playing hard to get or whether he was as yet unwilling to let go of the old animosities. I had hoped it was the former. As an "outsider," I was cautiously optimistic that Bar Pak could be won over.

More Dilemmas

"This is a collection of thieves and miscreants," Bar Pak said angrily after the meeting. "Why should I ever meet with this group of malcontents again?"

"You do not have to," replied Naseem. "Perhaps it is better to return to the old ways of violence, but I wonder who profits from that situation and who is harmed by it. Surely people will begin to ask why the insurgency has started again."

"That is simple, because Bala Khan has returned with his gang of thugs. Don't you think I know who you have been meeting with and who is biding his time in Mirgul?"

"We have nothing to hide," said Naseem calmly. "We have nothing to gain by working with these people . . . and nothing to lose."

"I will think about this." Bar Pak departed. This meeting had gone better than we had expected, but not as well as we had hoped.

"We need some leverage with Bar Pak," said Naseem. "His personal interests are too threatened and are clouding his judgment toward the Mir tribe."

The use of checks and balances, full financial transparency, and local ownership had seriously cut into Bar Pak's ability to extort or misappropriate aid and development money. As Naseem explained, government officials like Bar Pak "bought" their positions from the government on a semiannual basis. This purchase served as a sort of retainer for loyalty.

Bar Pak made the money back in part by "taxing" project funds or earning a fee by giving contracts to his friends and business associates. He would also purchase or seize land for the government, at either cut-rate prices or for free, and sell it at a significant profit. If he got fired, Bar Pak would lose his investment.

Right now, he was losing money. He was running the risk of being unable to pay the rent for his position.

"Al'a Dust, however, is politically useful," Naseem continued. "The president recognized his service during the Markhand wars. He does not need to buy his position. I did not have to either, because of my service. Many officials who earn their position honestly, however, will still participate in such practices. Some do it for more legitimate reasons, such as to create an operating budget for their organizations. Khanastan does not provide operations funding to provincial offices."

Meanwhile, the brigade's intelligence officers had associated the cell phone with Bala Khan's personal bodyguard. Various reports came to them and the special forces that Bala Khan was in Mirgul and was spending nights at three different houses.

I realized that we were in a race against the clock. Unless I could show something tangible that Bala Khan was giving up the fight, the brigade would organize a raid to kill or capture Bala Khan. Even if the raid was successful, it would destroy the relationship with the Mir tribe for good. We would go back to having one of the most violent areas of the country . . . or worse.

I argued that Bala Khan and his network were seriously considering reconciliation, as evidenced by the significant decrease in violence over the past two months. An operation now would permanently poison the well.

"Bala Khan is merely using this as a sham to buy time as he gathers more forces," said a member of the brigade staff. "You are being hood-winked. Special forces has a man on the inside reporting all of this to us."

The brigade commander seemed to agree with that assessment. "I appreciate your willingness to talk with the elders, but people like Bala Khan just need to be taken off the battlefield. Don't be fooled by these people. They have played foreigners for chumps before. Doing your own kinetic operation against him would at least let you control the outcome. Otherwise, I expect the SF to do it for you." The last comment was a veiled threat and showed what he thought of our approach.

I said we should consider who was actually getting played. "If Bala Khan were not serious, and if the Mir elders were just playing us, why would Bala Khan be in Mirgul rather than in Markhand 'gathering forces'? I know where all of these people live and have been to most of their homes—don't you think they could guess what would happen to them if this was only a ruse? There are plenty of people with an interest in derailing this initiative."

The brigade commander was not going to order me to stop engaging with the council or initiate an operation to kill or capture Bala Khan. That is not how he, or most people nowadays, operated. He would let the special operations effort run its course and not stop them. Either way, my pushback on this and our equally unconventional Zari efforts were earn-ing me a special place near bottom of the pecking order. He would not fire me, but he could ensure that I would not command at the next level if I persisted in the present course.

Perhaps I should just let this operation happen and return to operating in the conventional way, I thought. I could easily relent and say that I had to play devil's advocate to ensure we were right about a kinetic operation in Mirgul. Meanwhile, I had engineered a trap for Bala Khan and sprung it at just the right moment. Killing or capturing Bala Khan would be helpful to both of us in the eyes of our superiors. We were toward the end of the tour and would not have to deal with the fallout. And when I got to be a brigade commander, I could make sure my subordinates conducted counterinsurgency the way I had learned.

But if I stood on principle and sealed my fate, then I would never have the opportunity to impart to others what I had learned.

What was more important—standing on principle, knowing that it would probably end my chances of promotion and future command? Or bending on this issue now for a better chance to influence others down the road? Would I be the person I wanted to be in the future if I compromised on principle now?

Why was I only thinking about this now, twenty years into my career?

Understanding the Blood Feud— Protecting an Enemy From our Friends

Naseem arranged another meeting with the Mir elders at the Mirgul base and invited Bar Pak. Once again, the meeting was cordial.

I told the elders that I needed something tangible to prove that Bala Khan was going to stop fighting, and that without some sort of proof very soon, we risked losing the opportunity for peace. The elders said they needed more time. Bar Pak decided after the meeting that he was finished with the Mir council.

I was seriously worried that this entire effort was heading off the rails quickly. Naseem and his people had been working diligently to determine how information about Bala Khan's whereabouts was being reported and why. He had no idea that a raid was being contemplated.

Naseem believed that Mir Hamza, one of Bala Khan's subordinate leaders, was playing a double or triple game. He was the only one still alive who knew the circumstances of the attempted assassination of Al'a Dust. The others had either been killed in combat or died from unknown causes. Mir Hamza was from Qala Gul, the main village of the Nar tribe's Qala clan, which was friendly with the Mir. He and his family had moved to a village in Markhand. He played a key role in planning and logistical support for Bala Khan's forces.

According to Naseem's sources, Bala Khan had stayed at Mir Hamza's house the night prior to visiting Al'a Dust. Mir Hamza's men led Bala Khan to a linkup point in the mountains between Qala Gul and Baba Gul, where Al'a Dust's men met Bala Khan and escorted him and his three bodyguards to Al'a Dust's compound.

The Qala had long been friendly with the Mir tribe and at odds with the other clans of the Nar, particularly the powerful Dust clan. Certainly Mir Hamza had an interest in sustaining the feuding between the Nar and the Mir. He also had the most to lose in any sort of reconciliation between Bala Khan and Al'a Dust, or from an end to the fighting.

Naseem was far from any proof, however. Others had speculated the same theory, but Mir Hamza was fiercely loyal to Bala Khan and incredibly useful to him as well. Naseem needed to create some sort of test in which Mir Hamza would have to show himself as being against Bala Khan's wishes for peace. Naseem could never prove Mir Hamza's complicity, but he might be able to develop some way to undermine him and break his relationship with Bala Khan.

Naseem and I began to suspect that Bar Pak had been feeding information to the special forces and the Khanastan commandos. He did not support our efforts to reconcile with Bala Khan. He could maintain plausible deniability for any raid by reporting information through that channel, while staying somewhat engaged with the Mir council. He must have a source close enough to Bala Khan to gain information on his whereabouts.

We believed he kept the information from Al'a Dust, who probably would have taken matters into his own hands. If Mir Hamza was behind all of this, then he also had an interest in keeping the information from Al'a Dust, lest the latter suspect his complicity in starting the feud in the first place.

Naseem decided that he needed to gain some leverage over Bar Pak so that he would stop actively undermining the reconciliation effort with Bala Khan. Naseem had been gathering evidence for quite some time on Bar Pak's abuse of power and authority for personal gain. Although the Khanastan government had created the position-for-purchase system, they had begun, at the international community's insistence, cracking down on flagrant abuse of power. Khanastan had also insisted that the international community support efforts toward reconciliation.

Naseem requested a private meeting with Bar Pak in which they discussed reconciliation with Bala Khan. Bar Pak maintained his refusal to support the effort. Naseem said that Bar Pak could look like a hero in the eyes of the government if he became the first governor to bring a major insurgent leader to peace. Always motivated by personal gain and notoriety, Bar Pak began to sense that he might derive some benefit from such an outcome. He said he would think the matter over.

As he departed, Naseem gave him a packet and asked him to open it after he arrived back at the provincial center. I was not present at the meeting, but saw Naseem give the packet to Bar Pak at their parting.

Naseem recounted the meeting. I asked him what was in the packet.

"It contains evidence of Bar Pak's crimes against the people. I told him to open it after he returned to his office."

"What purpose will that serve?"

"Bar Pak is interested in personal gain only. He knows that unless he actively supports the reconciliation efforts with Bala Khan, I will turn over this evidence to the government. He will be finished. This will also help to curb some of his other abuses."

Bar Pak was losing financially from the transparency and checks and balances systems we had put in place. He probably would ask for a transfer soon to another place that would prove more lucrative. If he could do this while also gaining recognition for ending Bala Khan's insurgent activity, then he would be in a position for an even better job.

"Bar Pak is a thief. He has stolen from the people, but he is not a murderer. His crooked ways will catch up with him."

Naseem was a genius at gaining leverage over people. This effort was well into the gray area and I felt ill at ease about it, which is probably why he did not tell me about his plan beforehand. Nonetheless, it was the least bad alternative, and I accepted that.

As Naseem had suspected, Mir Hamza was Bar Pak's source of information. Bar Pak would not reveal that, but we received reports that Mir Hamza had left the area for Markhand a few days later. The reports of Bala Khan's whereabouts grew cold. The threat of a commando mission subsided.

Winning in Mirgul, Making Allies, Regaining Social and Political Balance

We now had some breathing space to determine whether reconciliation with Bala Khan was possible. Violence was almost nonexistent in the area. Confidence building with the Mir council had reached a point at which we could move toward integration of the Mir with the government.

With Bar Pak's grudging support, we created an integrated Nar and Mir council at the provincial level (the Zari tribe was not yet ready for this step). The council agreed to investigate the feud between Al'a Dust and Bala Khan, which meant all actions by each party against the other had to stop until the council made a ruling. Perhaps this was also an indication that Al'a Dust was becoming more open-minded about the incident.

We needed to integrate both tribes into the police as well, but that would require the support of Al'a Dust. This became possible once the council agreed to arbitrate the dispute.

A zarikai arrangement with the Mir would not be appropriate. Giving them a zarikai would require giving one to the Nar as well, and we did not want to risk creating rival militias. The compartmentalization of the terrain in the Zari areas and the relative independence of each village made zarikai a sensible arrangement there. Historically, that is how they defended themselves. There was no such tradition with the Nar and Mir. Integrating both tribes into the police made more sense.

Getting to that point first required a limited, conditional ceasefire. We needed to create greater confidence that the various sides could work together. If that effort held, we could then move forward on recruiting members of the Mir into the police force.

Al'a Dust was surprisingly easy to convince. He realized that his role as the chief of police was secure and that bringing the Mir on board would place him in a position of relative strength. Bala Khan, we had agreed, could play a role on the provincial council if he reconciled but he would not become a member of the security forces—either police or army.

We discussed options for the way forward with the Mir council. Naseem and I started the discussion by asking the elders to teach us how to say the words trust, friendship, respect, and peace in their dialect. We did the same for them in Naseem's dialect and in English. We wrote the words on whiteboards. I wrote in English and Naseem wrote in Khandu.

We wanted to shape the conversation and mentality of all present toward the significant step of a ceasefire.

We then divided up the whiteboards into four sections: the Mir, the government and coalition, Bala Khan, and the Takriri. We asked the council to state the main goals of the tribe. They cited peace, education, jobs, quality of life, and justice. We also asked them to state Bala Khan's goals, which were the same with the addition of coalition forces leaving the area.

We then asked them what they perceived to be our goals. They said they thought we wanted peace but also fighting. I think this meant they believed we wanted Bala Khan to surrender. They said our actions suggested that we also supported education, jobs, and quality of living, and we seemed to want justice but there was still too much corruption.

We clarified that we wanted peace "with dignity and honor for all sides," which satisfied their concern about surrender. We discussed the efforts we had made together toward improving corruption. I also stated that the coalition was interested in leaving as soon as possible, but that would only happen once durable peace was achieved.

Naseem stated that when people agree on eighty percent of the issues, that normally makes them allies.

We then asked what the Takriri wanted. They said such people wanted violence, poverty, control of the people, and lack of education. We agreed that those who wanted to prevent peace had goals contrary to the wishes of the rest of us, and that we needed to identify them and work together to counter their efforts.

With the mental shaping complete, we worked through an agreement for a limited, conditional ceasefire that included a "hot line" that would be monitored continuously in Mirgul and the surrounding villages and in joint command posts on the Narabad and Mirgul bases. This was designed to help prevent spoiler activity. The government and coalition forces were free to move throughout the area. House searches would be coordinated with the elders. All insurgent activity would cease, to include planning and coordination, IEDs, attacks, and "military movements"—the movement of fighters or equipment. We agreed to do no house raids unless the terms were violated or a threat existed. The agreement was in force for two weeks, at which time the terms could be revisited and extended.

Naseem and I were confident that word of this would get back to Bala Khan, and that he probably had already indicated support for the initiative. I was less worried about him at this point than about spoiler activity from Mir Hamza. We needed him to be isolated.

I got tremendous pushback on this from the brigade—one of the staff officers said we were surrendering to terrorists.

Nonetheless, the conditional ceasefire held for two weeks. At the next meeting, the Mir council arrived with a note from Bala Khan that he would not stop these efforts. That was all I needed to convince others to give the reconciliation efforts a chance.

Progress in Zari . . . and a New Set of Challenges

Meanwhile, the Zari area was continuing to improve. In Sher Wali's absence, we had gained a lot of momentum and concluded the commitment of mutual support with the Zari tribe. There were celebrations in the villages. I was beginning to think that we were over the hump.

But then Sher Wali returned from Markhand with a strong contingent of foreign fighters and a lot of money. He was no longer welcome in Pitigram, so he established a temporary base in a cave complex between Pitigram and Grond. He began an intimidation campaign, targeting the elders and zarikai in those villages.

We had been coordinating with the Zari elders to place an outpost near the village of Vala, which was halfway between Nishigram and Zargram, on the south side of the river near the road. We had the operation planned and all the resources lined up. But the Zari elders continued to ask for more time to try to solve the problem themselves.

Naseem and I had decided that with the combat power we had in reserve, we could emplace the outpost and still have the flexibility to conduct operations. With the Mir area progressing as well as it had been, we were more confident than ever in our ability to support a new outpost.

Zama and the hundred-man council remained convinced that they could bring Sher Wali's violence to a halt, but they did not count on him bringing reinforcements and having the ability to compete with the money we had committed to the area.

The hundred-man council held a meeting in Pitigram, but Sher Wali did not attend. They sent interlocutors into the mountains to meet with him, but the discussions came to nothing. Nonetheless, they were convinced a breakthrough was possible.

Naseem and I bided our time to let the council work but were prepared to jump on any action Sher Wali made indicating he was beyond the council's ability to control.

One evening, Sher Wali's men blew a wide hole in a bridge along the main road near Vala, threatening to cut off supplies to Zargram and other villages to the west and north.

At that point, Naseem and I put the operation into motion, establishing a base near Vala and three platoon-sized observation posts on the high ground—two on either side of the outpost and one on the north side of the river near Dadmuk.

The nighttime air assault to the observation posts went without incident, and the ground assault to Vala would follow a couple days later. We wanted the council's overt blessing for the position.

The elders were upset. Zama was furious, saying that one night's operation had destroyed months of work. They were on the cusp of an agreement, he said.

Naseem anticipated this. He expected the council to express public outrage that we had undermined their efforts but that they would privately support the matter, realizing that they were unable to control Sher Wali.

Naseem explained to them that regardless of what agreements Sher Wali did or did not make, he was responsible for blowing up the bridge. When the snows melted in the passes and the river rose, many villages in the area would be cut off from food. Sher Wali did this deliberately to try to punish the council and impose his will on the people.

He asked the council to accompany the ground assault to Vala. They initially refused, stating that they would have agreed to do so if we had not taken the observation posts first.

"I do not blame you," Zama said to me. "I blame him [Naseem] for giving you bad advice."

"We were left with no choice," said Naseem. "Once Sher Wali establishes his own positions overwatching the bridge, which is clearly his plan, you will be at his mercy. If that is what you want, then we will pull the positions out, and you can deal with Sher Wali yourself."

That was enough for the council to agree to accompany the patrol to Vala. Sher Wali had dishonored them and they knew it. They needed to mobilize their own people before Sher Wali was able to buy off the young men of Pitigram, Grond, and Margram, combine them with his foreign fighters, and then work his way toward Zargram.

We were in a race for time. Within ninety-six hours we had a reinforced perimeter established, complete with overhead cover and barrier and obstacle material. We kept the observation posts in place and patrolled relentlessly.

We put UAVs overhead and tried to nail down the cave complex where Sher Wali was hiding and potentially gathering forces. After one week, we lost the UAVs to another mission in a different area. We were blind north of the river except for reports from the people and what we could observe from the northern observation post.

Two weeks later, we held a meeting with the hundred-man council at the Vala outpost. I looked specifically for Ghani and other members of the Pitigram and Grond councils. They did not come. I asked Zama the reason for their absence. He said he did not know—he had seen them three days ago, and they said they had planned to come.

Zama spoke to the council and said that there were three powers in the district: the elders, the government, and the Takriri. While the term "Takriri" was often used by the coalition as synonymous with insurgents, we had learned over time to make distinctions. This was the first time Zama had used this term to describe Sher Wali's forces. Sher Wali had not been aligned with them before. Had he now turned to them for support? Naseem and I both noted the importance of this characterization.

Zama seemed to be intimating that the elders should agree to make war on the Takriri, which meant war on Sher Wali. Most were willing to do so, but without the main Bamal villages of Pitigram and Grond present, any decision could be twisted as war by the Salar against the Bamal.

Zama also kept his distance from me and Naseem during the event. We ate with different groups of people. He always had several elders around him, which made a private discussion impossible.

As the meeting was ending, Abdul Watan placed a note in my hand and indicated that he did not want me to look at it until everyone had left.

The Fight in Vala

I was concerned that Zama knew more than he indicated, and I was upset that he did not address the problem directly. The absence of the Pitigram and Grond councils probably meant that Sher Wali had intimidated them or even taken control of the area.

I showed Naseem the note, and his face darkened as he read it. "Expect a major attack this evening on the Vala base."

We got the UAV and fixed-wing support in place quickly. There was a little bit of crowing from the brigade staff about the council being a sham. If this were the case, however, we would not have received the warning.

Zama may have been keeping his distance during the meeting to give himself plausible deniability about tipping us off about the attack. He gave Abdul Watan that job—as a religious leader and a member of the Bamal clan, he would not be suspected.

I waited until nightfall to make adjustments to the perimeter defense, particularly the movement of additional heavy weapons and reinforcement of the positions. I was confident Sher Wali's scouts were watching and I did not want to give any indication that we had been tipped off.

Sher Wali's forces had only one good avenue of approach if they intended to overrun the base—that was from the south. Our observation posts flanked the base to the east and west and we had kept the northern outpost in position, so we should be able to identify an attack from the south while preventing a supporting attack from the north.

I suspected his plan would be to conduct supporting attacks against the observation posts to focus our attention there and try to assault the base using suicide bombers as a breaching force. Their best approach would be to stage the attack from the village. They would have to intimidate, overwhelm, or buy off the village zarikai to do that. Either way, large-scale insurgent occupation of the village would present several advantages to them and a lot of challenges for us. They could use the village as a sort of "human shield."

We needed to catch the main attack moving before they got near Vala. Had Sher Wali's force been primarily local fighters, they could infiltrate in small groups over a period of time and mass significant combat power without our knowing it. Their use of outsiders gave us an advantage, provided we could get to them before they got to the population.

With only one UAV and one fixed-wing sortie equipped with "sniper pods" that we could also use for surveillance, I focused on either side of the valley heading toward Vala. I kept the fighter aircraft at high altitude, out of audio range. Although this could degrade the resolution of their pods, we should be able to detect large movements and then reorient the UAV for positive identification.

Sher Wali would not be able to move all the way from Pitigram or Grond and then conduct an attack. He would have had to pre-position his forces. He undoubtedly timed this attack for that evening, after we met with the council, in an attempt to discredit them and sow suspicion among us. I do not doubt that a message got to Zama, probably that morning, threatening his family if he compromised the attack. That was why he refused to meet with Naseem and me alone.

I figured that the insurgents probably moved from a cave complex between Pitigram and Grond, then moved south and crossed the river somewhere between Nishigram and Vala, outside of our observation range. The loss of the UAV a week ago hurt badly—we might have been able to catch them moving from the cave complex.

If I guessed their crossing point correctly, they would move along a valley or ridgeline toward Vala that evening after most people had gone to bed. They could not afford to be seen due to the risk of compromise.

Sher Wali's forces could move far to the south of Vala and then work their way back up the valley toward the village, or they could move more directly along the ridgeline in a narrower arc outside the visual observation of our OP. I placed the surveillance assets to cover these two avenues.

Just after midnight, the UAV picked up a large formation of fighters moving along the valley floor about seven kilometers southwest of Vala. We counted around ninety of them. The large formation enabled us to gain AC-130 gunship support. Unfortunately, the two AC-130s would not arrive on station for another hour.

Two Apache attack helicopters were sent by the brigade, and we directed them toward the formation. They would arrive on station in twenty minutes, with only a one-hour time on station.

We decided to strike the formation with four two-thousand-pound laser-guided bombs—two at either end of the column and two toward the center. This would kill many of the attackers and trap the others in the valley. We would use the AH-64s to keep the survivors pinned down until the AC-130s arrived on station. We also had two hellfire missiles on the Predator.

We received two EA-12B electronic warfare aircraft. We gave them the frequencies commonly used by the insurgents to jam with "white noise"—if this was a coordinated attack, I wanted to ensure we did everything to disrupt their command and control.

The JTAC (Joint Tactical Air Controller) coordinated the points of impact with the two F-35 Joint Strike Fighters and issued the "Cleared Hot" after my approval. We only had one sniper pod feed in the small Vala command post. We could view the UAV feed on a different system. We tasked the UAV to focus on the front of the column and the sniper pod on the rear.

"Weapons release," announced the JTAC. "Thirty seconds to impact!"

"Ten seconds."

We held our breath, watching the two screens intently. The bomb at the head of the column detonated directly on target; the UAV observed for "squirters" (insurgents fleeing the scene). The two bombs toward the center of the column detonated as well with great effect. The fourth bomb, the one directed at the rear, was a dud. It hit a fighter directly on the chest but failed to explode.

We directed the AH-64s, which had just arrived on station, to focus on the back of the column. As the smoke cleared, about twenty insurgents raced southwest along the valley and directly into the 30-millimeter cannon and 2.75-inch rockets of the Apaches. Several of them attempted to take cover near or under rocks. The ones that ran were mowed down quickly.

One insurgent somehow survived the onslaught and raced down the valley footpath. His left arm was waving madly, as if it was nearly detached and now swinging uncontrollably due to the overall movement of the body. He was cut down in another gun run.

I was amazed at how many survived the initial bomb strike. Several insurgents toward the front of the column got up and began running toward Vala, only three kilometers away now. We needed to kill them before they reached the village.

The AC-130s arrived on station. We could not view the feed from their optics but watched the tracers from the 105-millimeter high-explosive rounds stream down from the sky and saw their effects through the UAV and sniper pod feeds. No insurgent came closer than two kilometers from the village. The AC-130 gunships then raked the rest of the column. They remained on station for one hour, enough time for the Apaches to refuel at the Nargul base and return to the fight.

The Apaches trolled the area for another ninety minutes while the F-35s refueled. There was no further movement along the valley floor or the adjacent mountains. I was not sure whether Sher Wali had been in the column or not. I suspected he had placed himself and a bodyguard in a position to control the fight away from the column itself.

My staff was busy with terrain analysis of possible command-and-control locations when a firefight erupted at the Nishigram outpost. We redirected the Apaches there while the UAV continued to scan likely command-and-control locations.

That firefight lasted about thirty minutes. After an initial volley of rocket-propelled grenades and machine gun fire, our soldiers dialed in on the insurgents very quickly to fix them in position while the Apaches got read-on and began their work.

The F-35s returned and were directed toward the Nishigram fight. We had only ten minutes left with the Apaches but another two hours of time with the F-35s.

As the F-35s were getting read-on, a firefight at the OP north of Vala began, as well as another smaller engagement on the OP east of Vala. With the Nishigram fight nearly over, we redirected the F-35s to support the Vala OPs. They were able to do split operations, with one F-35 supporting the northern OP and the other supporting the one to the east.

The northern OP was engaged in an intense firefight, so I retasked the UAV to support that action. The search for Sher Wali's command-and-control party would need to wait.

We coordinated the bomb drops from the F-35 and 155-millimeter artillery fire from the Nargul base. The fight at the northern OP lasted about one hour; the fight at the eastern OP ceased after the first five-hundred-pound bomb detonated.

Overall, we estimated that about 150 or more insurgents participated in the attacks—a very significant force. The ninety-man column was annihilated without being able to fire a shot; the others were defeated piecemeal. Attrition of the insurgents was substantial. We had one KNA soldier at the northern OP lightly wounded through the arm.

While we had beaten the insurgents badly, we needed to get Sher Wali. Given their use of obvious terrain in the various engagements, I guessed that these fighters were primarily outsiders—likely Takriris recruited from outside the province or from Markhand.

Sher Wali wanted to gain a tactical victory, sow suspicion between us and the Zari elders, and regain enough credibility that he could recruit more local fighters and restart the insurgency. He had failed to accomplish the first, and he would not accomplish the second. I was very concerned about thwarting the third goal. If people believed that the council supported the attack, or refused to warn us about it, then enough young men and women might believe that rejoining Sher Wali was acceptable.

My staff continued to request a second UAV and a replacement for the first before it went off station. We had already lost the F-35s to another area. I wanted to focus the UAVs on the suspected cave complex. If Sher Wali escaped, I suspected that he would make his way there.

An Unconventional Pursuit: Defeating the Zari Insurgency

I also wanted to keep Sher Wali out of Pitigram and Grond. I got approval for special forces and KNA commando missions to go to the two villages for medical and humanitarian assistance operations. Because of the deployment of the forces in and around Vala, I only had one platoon uncommitted that could provide a quick reaction force.

The approval took a lot of convincing. The brigade wanted to do cordon-and-search missions in the villages—which would have risked snatching defeat from the jaws of victory. Sher Wali wanted to sow mistrust, and a kinetic operation in those villages would have accomplished that. We wanted them to conduct the "softer" mission as a deterrent for Sher Wali while thanking "the people" for tipping us off about the attack.

To reinforce the message, we placed traffic-control points along the road outside the Nishigram and Vala bases—their job was to look for wounded fighters and thank all the passersby for the large volume of information we received warning us of the attack.

Sher Wali's attack was well-planned and done with great secrecy from the mountain hideout. He lost completely. I wanted to sow suspicion that the entire population had betrayed him, and that we had received a large volume of warnings.

The plan worked. We detected three groups of roughly ten people moving toward Pitigram and Grond and then dashing into the mountains. We could not detect any weapons from the UAV—they probably hid them under clothing—so we did not have positive identification of them as insurgents.

Nonetheless, we were able to follow them into the mountains until each group suddenly disappeared at the same point—most likely the cave complex. We withdrew the commando teams from Pitigram and Grond after successful missions there so they could refit for a follow-on mission to the caves. We kept the UAVs focused on the entrance and at other points on the mountain. We conducted routine "shows of force" in the area. We did not know if there were other entrances to or exits from the cave complex, so we wanted to discourage movement toward or away from the cave.

Three nights later, the special forces and KNA commandos struck the cave complex. I could not imagine a more difficult and dangerous mission and was thankful we had such incredible soldiers trained for these kinds of tasks.

The mission was executed perfectly. The commandos got close enough to the cave to provoke a firefight and then called in bomb strikes. AC-130s circled overhead while UAVs scanned for exits. One bomb hit the cave entrance perfectly. It was set on a time delay, so it would penetrate and then detonate. Part of the mountain face collapsed. The commandos entered a couple hours later.

The UAVs picked up a group of armed men emerging from another opening in the mountain. The AC-130s killed them. Sher Wali was among the thirty dead in the cave from the bomb strike; the remainder were fighters from Markhand and a handful of Sher Wali's local loyalists.

"Excellent!" shouted Alex as he came over to me. I was completely exhausted, having been in the simulation for more than twenty-four hours.

Mick came up to meet us. He was delighted with the results. "I had my doubts about what you were doing—and I'm still not convinced it would work in real life—but that was a terrific fight!"

We had a brief "hot wash" after-action review, then a more thorough review the next day.

Back to the Future

Alex and I met a month later. I had worked with my chain of command and soldiers on what I had learned from the simulation, and we had redesigned our approach to counterinsurgency. I was not foolish enough to believe that real life would resemble the simulation, but I was confident that if we had the basic mental models right we could adapt to the situation on the ground. I had all my officers and noncommissioned officers review each of the simulations so they had the same experience that I did. We then got as many soldiers as possible to see them as well.

Alex and I discussed the importance of social mobilization in defeating a local insurgency, the management of cost-benefit calculations, and the facilitation of local ownership and solutions. We exchanged views on ways to disrupt insurgent political cohesion by getting the ones fighting for practical reasons—the "reconcilables"—out of the fight so the irreconcilables would be marginalized, isolated, and more easily defeated.

I was pleased with the results but still questioned the durability of it all. At the point where I had ended the simulation, the Narabad government needed to be able to earn legitimacy. The system of checks and balances needed to be institutionalized to maintain public accountability. I was worried that, without reform at the central government, Bar Pak or his successor would find ways to undermine the system. As long as officials had to buy their positions, and do so at such exorbitant prices, there were powerful incentives toward corruption and abuse of power.

The government needed to get its public finance system fixed so it could function on its own. It also needed to provide the services, development, and economic opportunities that until now were primarily supported by us. I think the effort to force Bar Pak and his officials to use government funds rather than relying solely on our own was a step in the right direction. But unless the central government could consistently respond to demand signals from the provinces, this system would collapse as well.

Nonetheless, these advances that we had worked together so hard to put into place would need monitoring and follow-through to become fully operational. The work between the council and the government needed more time to become the "new normal." Old frictions and disputes would not simply go away—they needed to be resolved in a transparent and honest way. Spoilers would try to undermine these efforts.

"How are you going to deal with all that?" Alex asked.

"We'll need to communicate with our successor unit so they can pick up where we left off."

"Come take a look at something."

Alex led me to the control room, where Lieutenant Colonel John Safeway, the battalion commander whose unit would replace mine, was beginning the simulation. He had the advantage of being able to go through the simulation for the first time well over a year before his unit would deploy.

This first simulation experience would build on my simulation. He would go through the simulator again six months and three months before he deployed. Those simulations would be populated with data and information updates based on my unit's deployment.

As we looked down into the simulation room, we watched as he was fully briefed by a "virtual me" on what happened and why it happened, how we achieved the results that we did, and my recommended way forward. We had about a ten-day virtual handover. He listened politely and said he understood it all and was ready to go.

A couple days after the transfer of authority ceremony, he was approached by a man claiming that Bala Khan was planning an attack on the Mirgul base. A second man approached a day later with the same story.

"I knew this was all bullshit!" LTC Safeway exclaimed. "It's time to kill Bala Khan!"

ACKNOWLEDGMENTS

Counterinsurgency is extraordinarily difficult to do well—particularly in a vastly different society and culture. I do hope that our experiences in places such as Iraq and Afghanistan bring an added sense of humility toward such missions. This is not to say we should not engage in counterinsurgencies in the future—such sentiment would be dangerously naïve. We cannot always choose the kinds of conflicts or situations that threaten our national interests, but we can choose how we approach them and the extent to which we prepare our military forces and civilians to face them. I hope this book becomes a meaningful part of such preparation.

This book came about due to the hard work and dedication of many gifted professionals. I want to thank first my good friends at the Army War College Foundation, particularly Colonel (Retired) Ruth Collins, who have been wonderful partners in both my previous book, *Leadership: The Warrior's Art,* and in this work. I am very proud that proceeds from this book will support the educational mission of the Foundation.

I also want to thank the following people for the critical roles they played in shaping and refining my thinking for this book: Conrad Crane, a longtime friend and brilliant mentor; my insightful colleague and friend Nicole Kauss; and the wonderful people at Stackpole Books, especially Mark Allison and Kathryn Fulton.

Success has many mothers and fathers, to paraphrase an old saw, and this work is no different. I have had the privilege of learning from and commanding perhaps the finest group of counterinsurgents the Army has ever produced: 1st Squadron, 91st U.S. Cavalry (Airborne) of the 173rd Airborne Brigade. Commanding this incredible group of paratroopers for fifteen months in Afghanistan from 2007 to 2008 taught me what right looks like. Many of the lessons I learned are reflected in various ways throughout the text. In particular I would like to recognize my inner circle command team and staff: Vic Pedraza, Chris Doneski, Darren Fitz Gerald, Erik Berdy, Ted Kennedy, Kirk Dorr, Nathan Springer, John Williams, Dave Boris, Tim Kelly, Tom Bostick, Joey Hutto, Jason Pieri, Nick Talbot, Pete Gilbert, George Hughbanks, John Page, Dave Spencer, Adam King, Ben Kilgore, and Mike Sampsell.

After that deployment to Afghanistan, I was blessed to learn from some of the military's most senior leaders: Under Secretary Michèle Flournoy; Generals Stanley McChrystal, David Petraeus, David Rodriguez, and Terry Wolff; Admirals Michael Mullen and Sandy Winnefeld; Undersecretaries James Miller and Michael Vickers; and Mr. David Sedney. They were all instrumental in their own ways in developing my thinking on counterinsurgency. I want to thank, in particular, Michèle Flournoy for giving me the opportunity to apply my background to help her and the Obama Administration set a new strategic direction to the Afghan conflict, and General David Petraeus for the opportunity to work together with him on how to practice counterinsurgency in Afghanistan. Most importantly, I want to thank General Stan McChrystal for giving me the opportunity to serve on his team in Afghanistan, to lead the Strategic Assessment team, and to pen his counterinsurgency guidance. I am also deeply thankful for insights and inspiration from Greg Mortenson, Wakil Karimi, and Sarfraz Khan.

Finally, I want to thank Christine, Lauren, Mike, Zach, and Jake for their support and perseverance through extended deployments, significant trauma, and long hours at home as I attempted to capture what I have learned from those with whom I have served.